**Everyman's Poetry**

*Everyman, I will go with thee,
and be thy guide*

# The Open Road

## Poems on Travel

Selected and edited by STEPHEN PAIN

EVERYMAN
J. M. Dent · London

This edition published by Everyman Paperbacks in 2000
Selection, introduction and other critical apparatus
J. M. Dent 2000

J. M. Dent
Orion Publishing Group
Orion House
5 Upper St Martin's Lane
London WC2H 9EA

Typeset by Deltatype Ltd, Birkenhead, Merseyside
Printed in Great Britain by
The Guernsey Press Co. Ltd, Guernsey, C. I.

British Library Cataloguing-in-Publication
Data is available on request

ISBN 0 460 88214 7

# Contents

*Note on the Editor*   vi
*Introduction*   vii

## Poems

homer, *from* the Odyssey (as translated by George
    Chapman)   3
virgil, *from* The Aeneid (as translated by John Dryden)   14
ezra loomis pound, The Seafarer (from the early Anglo-
    Saxon text)   21
geoffrey chaucer, *from* The Canterbury Tales (from the
    General Prologue)   24
sir walter ralegh, The Passionate Man's Pilgrimage   29
michael drayton, To the Virginian Voyage   30
john donne, The Sun Rising   33
john donne, To Sir H. W. at His Going Ambassador to
    Venice   34
george turbeville, To Spencer   35
andrew marvell, Song of the Emigrants in Bermuda   38
mrs anne killigrew, On a Young Lady Whose Lord was
    Travelling   40
william cowper, The Solitude of Alexander Selkirk   41
lady mary wortley montagu, Written in the Chiosk of the
    British Palace, at Pera, Overlooking the City of
    Constantinople, Dec. 26, 1718 [1717]   43
mary robinson, Stanzas Written Between Dover and Calais,
    July 20, 1792   46
charlotte smith, *from* Beachy Head 1807 [comp. 1806]
  Cliffs in South-East England   48

samuel taylor coleridge, Kubla Khan
  Or, a Vision in a Dream. A Fragment  52
samuel taylor coleridge, France: An Ode  54
william wordsworth, Admonition to a Traveller  57
william wordsworth, England and Switzerland, 1802  58
william wordsworth, I Travell'd Among Unknown
     Men  58
william wordsworth, Lines Written a Few Miles Above
     Tintern Abbey, on Revisiting the Banks of the Wye
     During a Tour, July 13, 1798  59
percy bysshe shelley, Ozymandias of Egypt  63
percy bysshe shelley, Stanzas Written in Dejection –
     December 1818, Near Naples  64
percy bysshe shelley, Lines Written Among the Euganean
     Hills  65
george gordon byron, The Isles of Greece  70
fitz-greene halleck, Connecticut  73
fitz-greene halleck, Alnwick Castle  76
james clarence mangan, Siberia  80
william morris, Iceland First Seen  81
james thomson, In the Train  83
eugene field, In Amsterdam  84
henry charles beeching, Going Downhill on a Bicycle: A
     Boy's Song  86
walt whitman, Passage to India  87
walt whitman, To a Locomotive in Winter  96
oscar wilde, Impression du Voyage  97
oscar wilde, Rome Unvisited  98
amy levy, Ballade of an Omnibus  100
john godfrey saxe, Railroad Rhyme  101
matthew arnold, Stanzas From the Grande Chartreuse  104
robert louis stevenson, To an Island Princess  110
robert louis stevenson, To Kalakaua (With a present of a
     Pearl)  111
robert louis stevenson, To Princess Kaiulani  112
robert louis stevenson, To My Wife (A Fragment)  113

To Irina A. S.

# Note on the Editor

Stephen Pain is an Anglo-American writer and lecturer. He has taught both in England and Japan where he currently resides. He has edited several American classics for Everyman. His short stories and poetry have been published in several literary journals, including *New Poetry* (England) and *Redoubt* (Australia).

# Introduction

One of the more obvious themes of Western travel literature is that of the 'quest', which has its roots in many older cultures; in some initiation rituals to enable a young man to become a fully fledged member of the tribe he must set off on a solitary journey into the wilderness. After a specific length of time or after a task has been carried out, he may then take his place within the tribe.

The first poems in this anthology, extracts from Homer and Virgil, are examples of a hero on a quest. In Homer's *Odyssey* the hero Odysseus (or Ulysses as he is also known), a veteran of the Trojan Wars, escapes from an island – where he has been held captive by the beautiful Calypso – to return home to his wife, Penelope. The *Odyssey* could be subtitled 'home-coming' or 'the return' as this is central to the narrative. Virgil's *Aeneid*, on the other hand, a Latin cover version of the *Odyssey* and the *Iliad*, is about Aeneas's quest to find a place to settle. Both authors were well travelled, Homer earning the nickname 'Wanderer', and Virgil travelling widely to research for his poetry. Indeed, travel was the cause of Virgil's death, as he succumbed to fever while travelling. On their journeys both Odysseus and Aeneas face many difficulties and hazards. Interestingly, one of the major hazards in the epics is a moral one; the men are tempted by Calypso and Dido. Their responses might differ but generally both heroes reject the advances of these women. In the case of the *Aeneid* it leads to tragedy.

Resting somewhere between the quest and pilgrimage, the Anglo-Saxon poem 'The Seafarer' is an example of the work of a voluntary exile. The Ezra Pound translation, which is included here, though perhaps not considered technically the best is arguably the most satisfying from an aesthetic point of view. Assisted by the use of alliteration, it conveys much of the mood of the original – loneliness in a harsh environment. Some critics see the poem as mirroring the story of Christ or the development of the Christian Church. The poem is packed with observations that suggest the author had a keen eye and, arguably, the seascape in the poem could be read in the same way that a young Native American might read the landscape.

Another important theme that influences travel verse is that of the pilgrimage, or making a journey to a sacred place as an act of devotion. The next poem, an extract from the General Prologue to *The Canterbury Tales*, is an example of this. The tales follow the pilgrimage route from the Tabard Inn at Southwark (the secular world) to Canterbury Cathedral, the most holy place in England, a shrine that held the body of St Augustine and the location of the martyrdom of Thomas à Becket (1170). The tales are each told by one of the pilgrims, each containing a moral and ranging from the chivalric tale of the knight to the very bawdy tale of the worldly miller. Although the poem is written in the vernacular, in English rather than Latin, it contains many allusions to the classical world, and the cosmopolitan nature of the author and his milieu is evident. In the wider world the most sacred place for Christians was Jerusalem and the journey there was undertaken by many thousands, particularly by soldiers during the Crusades, but also by groups of pilgrims.

The Renaissance provides us with another theme, that of exploration. Many writers of poetry in this period wrote of or went on expeditions to the Americas, North Africa and elsewhere. During this time map-making became important and entire continents were newly discovered by Europeans. The chief motivation for exploration was the search for the Promised Land and for that fabled place of unlimited riches, El Dorado. Sir Walter Ralegh, Queen Elizabeth's favourite courtier, travelled on several expeditions to the Americas, eventually laying claim to Guiana in South America. Most of these expeditions included piracy and skirmishes with other maritime powers like Spain, Holland and Portugal. It was after one expedition to the Orinoco that Ralegh returned without gold – it cost him his life.

Noticeably, Michael Drayton's poem 'To the Virginian Voyage' describing the voyage to the New World is laden with biblical allusions and imagery. People at the time often viewed the world in strictly religious terms and named places after places in the Bible. The language and imagery of discovery and exploration – equipment such as astrolabes, dividers, compasses and so on – became assimilated into the political satires and love poems of the metaphysical poets, such as John Donne (1572–1631).

In many ways, the eighteenth century saw the consolidation of capitalism and colonialism, some changes in the distribution of wealth, and a rise in the importance of science. These changes, in combination with improvements in transportation, led to the idea of travel as having a pedagogical function. Topographical verse boomed, and the Grand Tour to Europe was born. It became a rite of passage for the young nobleman, and a matter of necessity for anyone interested in the humanities, giving the opportunity of seeing classical sites at first hand. It also marks a second stage in the origins of tourism: now instead of the relics of St Francis of Assisi the traveller brought back paintings, engravings and furniture from Italy and France.

The Romantic period saw the greatest number of poet travellers: the Lake poets, Byron, Shelley and many others. They made pilgrimages to natural places of beauty and to lonely or remote locations, the purpose of which was perhaps more pantheistic, as it was a mixture of the spiritual, aesthetic and natural, something akin to what drives the New Age traveller to Glastonbury or Bali. During the same period the idea of the 'aesthetic' developed as well as theories of beauty and the parallel interest in the landscape as an object of art. This was given philosophical support by Edmund Burke's theory on the sublime. William Gilpin wrote on the idea of the picturesque in three essays: 'On Picturesque Beauty', 'On Picturesque Travel' and 'Sketching Landscape' (1792). Wordsworth's poem 'Lines Written a Few Miles Above Tintern Abbey' or Fitz-Greene Halleck's 'Alnwick Castle' are influenced by these ideas:

> Gaze on the Abbey's ruined pile:
>     Does not the succoring ivy, keeping
> Her watch around it, seem to smile,
>     As o'er a loved one sleeping?
> One solitary turret gray
>     Still tells, in melancholy glory,
> The legend of the Cheviot day,
>     The Percys' proudest border story.

Travel literature is problematic, perhaps more so than any other category of literature, because the act of travelling is often one that involves crossing cultural boundaries and may mean coming face to face with people of different cultures, often on unequal terms, as during the periods of colonialism. Also, it is usually gender-specific. In the *Odyssey* it is poor Penelope who must await the return of her husband Odysseus from his adventures. Moreover, Odysseus rejects Calypso and Circe and implicit in his rejection is that common xenophobic prejudice that foreign women have more carnal knowledge or experience than the women of one's own country.

In English poetry the image of the White Cliffs of Dover occurs frequently because to leave England was to leave behind home and all that home means. The rough crossing over to the Continent was a metaphor for the social and cultural risks involved in transculturation. Mary Robinson, however, recently estranged from her husband, turns the crossing into a personal allegory in her poem 'Stanzas Written Between Dover and Calais, July 20, 1792':

> Bounding billow, cease thy motion,
> Bear me not so swiftly o'er;
> Cease thy roaring, foamy ocean,
> I will tempt thy rage no more.

Another woman writer, Lady Mary Wortley Montagu (1689–1762), spent many years living abroad. It was during a stay in Turkey that she wrote letters and poetry about life in the harem, a place out of bounds for males. Her poem 'Written in the Chiosk of the British Palace, at Pera, Overlooking the City of Constantinople, Dec. 26, 1718 [1717]' offers the reader a beautiful comparison between the climates of England and Turkey:

> Ev'n Thames, benumb'd, 's a river now no more:
> The barren meads no longer yield delight,
> By glist'ning snows made painful to the sight.
> Here summer reigns with one eternal smile,
> Succeeding harvests bless the happy soil;

Not surprisingly, hundreds of books were published on the subject of 'advice' to travellers, much of it warnings, and the target market was mainly untravelled women. Right up until the beginning of the twentieth century, for a woman to breach travel etiquette, to go unchaperoned, and travel without a Baedeker guide book, was symptomatic of a deeper rebellion, of a proto-suffragism. Yet at the same time, for men there was a popular underground literature for those who wanted to sow their wild oats during their travels. Robert Louis Stevenson's, and the artist Paul Gauguin's, love for Polynesia could be read as a variant of this.

Recently, the travel writer Colin Thubron has travelled to Siberia, a place that has always fascinated me, and more so after I flew with Aeroflot over the vast wasteland of frozen lakes and rivers. It was for that reason I chose a poem by the Anglo-Irish poet and patriot, James Clarence Mangan (1803–49), 'Siberia':

> In Siberia's wastes
> Are sands and rocks,
> Nothing blooms of green or soft,
> But the snow-peaks rise aloft
> And the gaunt ice-blocks.

While the poem is ostensibly about the Siberia to which political dissidents and criminals were exiled, that frozen hell which is even talked of today, the desolate tone of the poem is the hallmark of Mangan, a poetic reflection of his own troubled psyche, reminding us in the end that all geographies and travel verse are indeed imagined and come from deep within us. Bon voyage.

stephen pain

# The Open Road

# HOMER

# from **The Odyssey**

(as translated by George Chapman)

I am Ulysses Laertiades,
The fear of all the world for policies,
For which my facts as high as heaven resound.
I dwell in Ithaca, earth's most renown'd,
All over-shadow'd with the shake-leaf hill,
Tree-famed Neritus; whose near confines fill
Islands a number, well inhabited,
That under my observance taste their bread;
Dulichius, Samos, and the full-of-food
Zacynthus, likewise graced with store of wood.
But Ithaca, though in the seas it lie,
Yet lies she so aloft she casts her eye
Quite over all the neighbour continent;
Far northward situate, and, being lent
But little favour of the morn and sun,
With barren rocks and cliffs is over-run,
And yet of hardy youths a nurse of name;
Nor could I see a soil, where'er I came,
More sweet and wishful. Yet, from hence was I
Withheld with horror by the Deity,
Divine Calypso, in her cavy house,
Enflamed to make me her sole lord and spouse.
Circe Aaa too, that knowing dame,
Whose veins the like affections did enflame,
Detain'd me likewise. But to neither's love
Could I be tempted; which doth well approve,
Nothing so sweet is as our country's earth,
And joy of those from whom we claim our birth.
Though roofs far richer we far off possess,
Yet, from our native, all our more is less.
    To which as I contended, I will tell

The much-distress-conferring facts that fell
By Jove's divine prevention, since I set
From ruin'd Troy my first foot in retreat.
   From Ilion ill winds cast me on the coast
The Cicons hold, where I employ'd mine host
For Ismarus, a city built just by
My place of landing; of which victory
Made me expugner. I depeopled it,
Slew all the men, and did their wives remit,
With much spoil taken; which we did divide,
That none might need his part. I then applied
All speed for flight; but my command therein,
Fools that they were, could no observance win
Of many soldiers, who, with spoil fed high,
Would yet fill higher, and excessively
Fell to their wine, gave slaughter on the shore
Cloven-footed beeves and sheep in mighty store.
In mean space, Cicons did to Cicons cry,
When, of their nearest dwellers, instantly
Many and better soldiers made strong head,
That held the continent, and managed
Their horse with high skill, on which they would fight,
When fittest cause served, and again alight,
With soon seen vantage, and on foot contend.
Their concourse swift was, and had never end;
As thick and sudden 'twas, as flowers and leaves
Dark spring discovers, when she light receives.
And then began the bitter Fate of Jove
To alter us unhappy, which even strove
To give us suff'rance. At our fleet we made
Enforced stand; and there did they invade
Our thrust-up forces; darts encounter'd darts,
With blows on both sides; either making parts
Good upon either, while the morning shone,
And sacred day her bright increase held on,
Though much out-match'd in number; but as soon
As Phoebus westward fell, the Cicons won
Much hand of us; six proved soldiers fell,
Of every ship, the rest they did compel
To seek of Flight escape from Death and Fate.

Thence sad in heart we sail'd; and yet our state
Was something cheer'd, that (being o'er-match'd so much
In violent number) our retreat was such
As saved so many. Our dear loss the less,
That they survived, so like for like success.
Yet left we not the coast, before we call'd
Home to our country earth the souls exhal'd
Of all the friends the Cicons overcame.
Thrice call'd we on them by their several name,
And then took leave. Then from the angry North
Cloud-gathering Jove a dreadful storm call'd forth
Against our navy, cover'd shore and all
With gloomy vapours. Night did headlong fall
From frowning heaven. And then hurl'd here and there
Was all our navy; the rude winds did tear
In three, in four parts, all their sails; and down
Driven under hatches were we, prest to drown.
Up rush'd we yet again, and with tough hand
(Two days, two nights, entoil'd) we gat near land,
Labours and sorrows eating up our minds.
The third clear day yet, to more friendly winds
We masts advanced, we white sails spread, and sate.
Forewinds and guides again did iterate
Our ease and home-hopes; which we clear had reach'd,
Had not, by chance, a sudden north-wind fetch'd,
With an extreme sea, quite about again
Our whole endeavours, and our course constrain
To giddy round, and with our bow'd sails greet
Dreadful Maleia, calling back our fleet
As far forth as Cythera. Nine days more
Adverse winds toss'd me; and the tenth, the shore,
Where dwelt the blossom-fed Lotophagi,
I fetch'd, fresh water took in, instantly
Fell to our food aship-board, and then sent
Two of my choice men to the continent
(Adding a third, a herald) to discover
What sort of people were the rulers over
The land next to us. Where, the first they met,
Were the Lotophagi, that made them eat
Their country diet, and no ill intent

Hid in their hearts to them; and yet th' event
To ill converted it, for, having eat
Their dainty viands, they did quite forget
(As all men else that did but taste their feast)
Both countrymen and country, nor address'd
Any return t' inform what sort of men
Made fix'd abode there, but would needs maintain
Abode themselves there, and eat that food ever.
I made out after, and was feign to sever
Th' enchanted knot by forcing their retreat,
That strived, and wept, and would not leave their meat
For heaven itself. But, dragging them to fleet,
I wrapt in sure bands both their hands and feet,
And cast them under hatches, and away
Commanded all the rest without least stay,
Lest they should taste the lote too, and forget
With such strange raptures their despised retreat.
     All then aboard, we beat the sea with oars,
     And still with sad hearts sail'd by out-way shores,
Till th' out-law'd Cyclops' land we fetch'd; a race
Of proud-lived loiterers, that never sow;
Nor put a plant in earth, nor use a plow,
But trust in God for all things; and their earth,
Unsown, unplow'd, gives every offspring birth
That other lands have; wheat, and barley, vines
That bear in goodly grapes delicious wines;
And Jove sends showers for all. No counsels there,
Nor counsellors, nor laws; but all men bear
Their heads aloft on mountains, and those steep,
And on their tops too; and their houses keep
In vaulty caves, their households govern'd all
By each man's law, imposed in several,
Nor wife, nor child awed, but as he thinks good,
None for another caring. But there stood
Another little isle, well stored with wood,
Betwixt this and the entry; neither nigh
The Cyclops' isle, nor yet far off doth lie.
Men's want it suffer'd, but the men's supplies
The goats made with their inarticulate cries.
Goats beyond number this small island breeds,

So tame, that no access disturbs their feeds,
No hunters, that the tops of mountains scale,
And rub through woods with toil, seek them at all.
Nor is the soil with flocks fed down, nor plow'd,
Nor ever in it any seed was sow'd.
Nor place the neighbour Cyclops their delights
In brave vermilion-prow-deck'd ships; nor wrights
Useful, and skilful in such works as need
Perfection to those traffics that exceed
Their natural confines, to fly out and see
Cities of men, and take in mutually
The prease of others; to themselves they live,
And to their island that enough would give
A good inhabitant; and time of year
Observe to all things art could order there.
There, close upon the sea, sweet meadows spring,
That yet of fresh streams want no watering
To their soft burthens, but of special yield.
Your vines would be there; and your common field
But gentle work make for your plow, yet bear
A lofty harvest when you came to shear;
For passing fat the soil is. In it lies
A harbour so opportune, that no ties,
Halsers, or gables need, nor anchors cast.
Whom storms put in there are with stay embraced,
Or to their full wills safe, or winds aspire
To pilots' uses their more quick desire.
   At entry of the haven, a silver ford
   Is from a rock-impressing fountain pour'd,
All set with sable poplars. And this port
Were we arrived at, by the sweet resort
Of some God guiding us, for 'twas a night
So ghastly dark all port was past our sight,
Clouds hid our ships, and would not let the moon
Afford a beam to us, the whole isle won
By not an eye of ours. None thought the blore,
That then was up, shov'd waves against the shore,
That then to an unmeasured height put on;
We still at sea esteem'd us, till alone
Our fleet put in itself. And then were strook

Our gather'd sails; our rest ashore we took,
And day expected. When the morn gave fire,
We rose, and walk'd, and did the isle admire;
The Nymphs, Jove's daughters, putting up a herd
Of mountain goats to us, to render cheer'd
My fellow soldiers. To our fleet we flew,.
Our crooked bows took, long-piled darts, and drew
Ourselves in three parts out; when, by the grace
That God vouchsafed, we made a gainful chace.
Twelve ships we had, and every ship had nine
Fat goats allotted [it], ten only mine.
Thus all that day, even till the sun was set,
We sat and feasted, pleasant wine and meat
Plenteously taking; for we had not spent
Our ruddy wine aship-board, supplement
Of large sort each man to his vessel drew,
When we the sacred city overthrew
That held the Cicons. Now then saw we near
The Cyclops' late-praised island, and might hear
The murmur of their sheep and goats, and see
Their smokes ascend. The sun then set, and we,
When night succeeded, took our rest ashore.
And when the world the morning's favour wore,
I call'd my friends to council, charging them
To make stay there, while I took ship and stream,
With some associates, and explored what men
The neighbour isle held; if of rude disdain,
    Churlish and tyrannous, or minds bewray'd
    Pious and hospitable. Thus much said,
I boarded, and commanded to ascend
My friends and soldiers, to put off, and lend
Way to our ship. They boarded, sat, and beat
The old sea forth, till we might see the seat
The greatest Cyclop held for his abode,
Which was a deep cave, near the common road
Of ships that touch'd there, thick with laurels spread,
Where many sheep and goats lay shadowed;
And, near to this, a hall of torn-up stone,
High built with pines, that heaven and earth attone,
And lofty-fronted oaks; in which kept house

A man in shape immane, and monsterous,
Fed all his flocks alone, nor would afford
Commerce with men, but had a wit abhorr'd,
His mind his body answering. Nor was he
Like any man that food could possibly
Enhance so hugely, but, beheld alone,
Show'd like a steep hill's top, all overgrown
With trees and brambles; little thought had I
Of such vast objects. When, arrived so nigh,
Some of my loved friends I made stay aboard,
To guard my ship, and twelve with me I shored,
The choice of all. I took besides along
A goat-skin flagon of wine, black and strong,
That Maro did present, Evantheus' son,
And priest to Phoebus, who had mansion
In Thracian Ismarus (the town I took)
He gave it me, since I (with reverence strook
Of his grave place, his wife and children's good)
Freed all of violence. Amidst a wood,
Sacred to Phoebus, stood his house; from whence
He fetch'd me gifts of varied excellence;
Seven talents of fine gold; a bowl all framed
Of massy silver; but his gift most famed
Was twelve great vessels, fill'd with such rich wine
As was incorruptible and divine.
He kept it as his jewel, which none knew
But he himself, his wife, and he that drew.
It was so strong, that never any fill'd
A cup, where that was but by drops instill'd,
And drunk it off, but 'twas before allay'd
With twenty parts in water; yet so sway'd
The spirit of that little, that the whole
A sacred odour breath'd about the bowl.
Had you the odour smelt and scent it cast,
It would have vex'd you to forbear the taste.
But then, the taste gain'd too, the spirit it wrought
To dare things high set up an end my thought.
    Of this a huge great flagon full I bore,
And, in a good large knapsack, victuals store;
And long'd to see this heap of fortitude,

That so illiterate was and upland rude
That laws divine nor human he had learn'd.
With speed we reach'd the cavern; nor discern'd
His presence there, his flocks he fed at field.
　　Ent'ring his den, each thing beheld did yield
Our admiration; shelves with cheeses heap'd;
Sheds stuff'd with lambs and goats, distinctly kept,
Distinct the biggest, the more mean distinct,
Distinct the youngest. And in their precinct,
Proper and placeful, stood the troughs and pails,
In which he milk'd; and what was given at meals,
Set up a creaming; in the evening still
All scouring bright as dew upon the hill.
　　Then were my fellows instant to convey
Kids, cheeses, lambs, aship-board, and away
Sail the salt billow. I thought best not so,
But better otherwise; and first would know,
What guest-gifts he would spare me. Little knew
My friends on whom they would have prey'd. His view
Prov'd after, that his inwards were too rough
For such bold usage. We were bold enough
In what I suffer'd; which was there to stay,
Make fire and feed there, though bear none away.
There sat we, till we saw him feeding come,
And on his neck a burthen lugging home,
Most highly huge, of sere-wood, which the pile
That fed his fire supplied all supper-while.
Down by his den he threw it, and up rose
A tumult with the fall. Afraid, we close
Withdrew ourselves, while he into a cave
Of huge receipt his high-fed cattle drave,
All that he milk'd; the males he left without
His lofty roofs, that all bestrow'd about
With rams and buck-goats were. And then a rock
He lift aloft, that damm'd up to his flock
The door they enter'd; 'twas so hard to wield,
That two and twenty waggons, all four-wheel'd,
(Could they be loaded, and have teams that were
Proportion'd to them) could not stir it there.
Thus making sure, he kneel'd and milk'd his ewes,

And braying goats, with all a milker's dues;
Then let in all their young. Then quick did dress
His half milk up for cheese, and in a press
Of wicker press'd it; put in bowls the rest,
To drink and eat, and serve his supping feast.
　　All works dispatch'd thus, he began his fire;
Which blown, he saw us, and did thus inquire:
　　'Ho! guests! What are ye? Whence sail ye these seas?
Traffic, or rove ye, and like thieves oppress
Poor strange adventurers, exposing so
Your souls to danger, and your lives to woe?'
　　This utter'd he, when fear from our hearts took
The very life, to be so thunder-strook
With such a voice, and such a monster see;
But thus I answer'd: 'Erring Grecians, we
From Troy were turning homewards, but by force
Of adverse winds, in far diverted course,
Such unknown ways took, and on rude seas toss'd,
As Jove decreed, are cast upon this coast.
Of Agamemnon, famous Atreus' son,
We boast ourselves the soldiers; who hath won
Renown that reacheth heaven, to overthrow
So great a city, and to ruin so
So many nations. Yet at thy knees lie
Our prostrate bosoms, forced with prayers to try
If any hospitable right, or boon
Of other nature, such as have been won
By laws of other houses, thou wilt give.
Reverence the Gods, thou great'st of all that live.
We suppliants are; and hospitable Jove
Pours wreak on all whom prayers want power to move,
And with their plagues together will provide
That humble guests shall have their wants supplied.'
　　He cruelly answer'd: 'O thou fool,' said he,
'To come so far, and to importune me
With any God's fear, or observed love!
We Cyclops care not for your goat-fed Jove,
Nor other Bless'd ones; we are better far.
To Jove himself dare I bid open war,
To thee, and all thy fellows, if I please.

But tell me, where's the ship, that by the seas
Hath brought thee hither? If far off, or near,
Inform me quickly.' These his temptings were;
But I too much knew not to know his mind,
And craft with craft paid, telling him the wind
(Thrust up from sea by Him that shakes the shore)
Had dash'd our ships against his rocks, and tore
Her ribs in pieces close upon his coast,
And we from high wrack saved, the rest were lost.
  He answer'd nothing, but rush'd in, and took
Two of my fellows up from earth, and strook
Their brains against it. Like two whelps they flew
About his shoulders, and did all embrue
The blushing earth. No mountain lion tore
Two lambs so sternly, lapp'd up all their gore
Gush'd from their torn-up bodies, limb by limb
(Trembling with life yet) ravish'd into him.
Both flesh and marrow-stuffed bones he eat,
And even th' uncleansed entrails made his meat.
We, weeping, cast our hands to heaven, to view
A sight so horrid. Desperation flew,
With all our after lives, to instant death,
In our believed destruction. But when breath
The fury of his appetite had got,
Because the gulf his belly reach'd his throat,
Man's flesh, and goat's milk, laying layer on layer,
Till near choked up was all the pass for air,
Along his den, amongst his cattle, down
He rush'd, and streak'd him. When my mind was grown
Desperate to step in, draw my sword, and part
His bosom where the strings about the heart
Circle the liver, and add strength of hand.
But that rash thought, more stay'd, did countermand,
For there we all had perish'd, since it past
Our powers to lift aside a log so vast,
As barr'd all outscape; and so sigh'd away
The thought all night, expecting active day.
Which come, he first of all his fire enflames,
Then milks his goats and ewes, then to their dams
Lets in their young, and, wondrous orderly,

With manly haste dispatch'd his housewifery.
Then to his breakfast, to which other two
Of my poor friends went; which eat, out then go
His herds and fat flocks, lightly putting by
The churlish bar, and closed it instantly;
For both those works with ease as much he did,
As you would ope and shut your quiver lid.
   With storms of whistlings then his flock he drave
Up to the mountains; and occasion gave
For me to use my wits, which to their height
I strived to screw up, that a vengeance might
By some means fall from thence, and Pallas now
Afford a full ear to my neediest vow.
This then my thoughts preferr'd: A huge club lay
Close by his milk-house, which was now in way
To dry and season, being an olive-tree
Which late he fell'd, and, being green, must be
Made lighter for his manage. 'Twas so vast,
That we resembled it to some fit mast,
To serve a ship of burthen that was driven
With twenty oars, and had a bigness given
To bear a huge sea. Full so thick, so tall,
We judg'd this club; which I, in part, hew'd small,
And cut a fathom off. The piece I gave
Amongst my soldiers, to take down, and shave;
Which done, I sharpen'd it at top, and then,
Harden'd in fire, I hid it in the den
Within a nasty dunghill reeking there,
Thick, and so moist it issued everywhere.
Then made I lots cast by my friends to try
Whose fortune served to dare the bored out eye
Of that man-eater; and the lot did fall
On four I wish'd to make my aid of all,
And I the fifth made, chosen like the rest.

## VIRGIL

# from **The Aeneid**

(as translated by John Dryden)

Arms, and the man I sing, who, forc'd by fate,
And haughty Juno's unrelenting hate,
Expell'd and exil'd, left the Trojan shore.
Long labors, both by sea and land, he bore,
And in the doubtful war, before he won
The Latian realm, and built the destin'd town;
His banish'd gods restor'd to rites divine,
And settled sure succession in his line,
From whence the race of Alban fathers come,
And the long glories of majestic Rome.
O Muse! the causes and the crimes relate;
What goddess was provok'd, and whence her hate;
For what offense the Queen of Heav'n began
To persecute so brave, so just a man;
Involv'd his anxious life in endless cares,
Expos'd to wants, and hurried into wars!
Can heav'nly minds such high resentment show,
Or exercise their spite in human woe?
Against the Tiber's mouth, but far away,
An ancient town was seated on the sea;
A Tyrian colony; the people made
Stout for the war, and studious of their trade:
Carthage the name; belov'd by Juno more
Than her own Argos, or the Samian shore.
Here stood her chariot; here, if Heav'n were kind,
The seat of awful empire she design'd.
Yet she had heard an ancient rumor fly,
(Long cited by the people of the sky,)
That times to come should see the Trojan race
Her Carthage ruin, and her tow'rs deface;
Nor thus confin'd, the yoke of sov'reign sway
Should on the necks of all the nations lay.

She ponder'd this, and fear'd it was in fate;
Nor could forget the war she wag'd of late
For conqu'ring Greece against the Trojan state.
Besides, long causes working in her mind,
And secret seeds of envy, lay behind;
Deep graven in her heart the doom remain'd
Of partial Paris, and her form disdain'd;
The grace bestow'd on ravish'd Ganymed,
Electra's glories, and her injur'd bed.
Each was a cause alone; and all combin'd
To kindle vengeance in her haughty mind.
For this, far distant from the Latian coast
She drove the remnants of the Trojan host;
And sev'n long years th' unhappy wand'ring train
Were toss'd by storms, and scatter'd thro' the main.
Such time, such toil, requir'd the Roman name,
Such length of labor for so vast a frame.
Now scarce the Trojan fleet, with sails and oars,
Had left behind the fair Sicilian shores,
Ent'ring with cheerful shouts the wat'ry reign,
And plowing frothy furrows in the main;
When, lab'ring still with endless discontent,
The Queen of Heav'n did thus her fury vent:
'Then am I vanquish'd? must I yield?' said she,
'And must the Trojans reign in Italy?
So Fate will have it, and Jove adds his force;
Nor can my pow'r divert their happy course.
Could angry Pallas, with revengeful spleen,
The Grecian navy burn, and drown the men?
She, for the fault of one offending foe,
The bolts of Jove himself presum'd to throw:
With whirlwinds from beneath she toss'd the ship,
And bare expos'd the bosom of the deep;
Then, as an eagle gripes the trembling game,
The wretch, yet hissing with her father's flame,
She strongly seiz'd, and with a burning wound
Transfix'd, and naked, on a rock she bound.
But I, who walk in awful state above,
The majesty of heav'n, the sister wife of Jove,
For length of years my fruitless force employ

Against the thin remains of ruin'd Troy!
What nations now to Juno's pow'r will pray,
Or off'rings on my slighted altars lay?'
Thus rag'd the goddess; and, with fury fraught.
The restless regions of the storms she sought,
Where, in a spacious cave of living stone,
The tyrant Aeolus, from his airy throne,
With pow'r imperial curbs the struggling winds,
And sounding tempests in dark prisons binds.
This way and that th' impatient captives tend,
And, pressing for release, the mountains rend.
High in his hall th' undaunted monarch stands,
And shakes his scepter, and their rage commands;
Which did he not, their unresisted sway
Would sweep the world before them in their way;
Earth, air, and seas thro' empty space would roll,
And heav'n would fly before the driving soul.
In fear of this, the Father of the Gods
Confin'd their fury to those dark abodes,
And lock'd 'em safe within, oppress'd with mountain loads;
Impos'd a king, with arbitrary sway,
To loose their fetters, or their force allay.
To whom the suppliant queen her pray'rs address'd,
And thus the tenor of her suit express'd:
'O Aeolus! for to thee the King of Heav'n
The pow'r of tempests and of winds has giv'n;
Thy force alone their fury can restrain,
And smooth the waves, or swell the troubled main –
A race of wand'ring slaves, abhorr'd by me,
With prosp'rous passage cut the Tuscan sea;
To fruitful Italy their course they steer,
And for their vanquish'd gods design new temples there.
Raise all thy winds; with night involve the skies;
Sink or disperse my fatal enemies.
Twice sev'n, the charming daughters of the main,
Around my person wait, and bear my train:
Succeed my wish, and second my design;
The fairest, Deiopeia, shall be thine,
And make thee father of a happy line.'
To this the god: "T'is yours, O queen, to will

The work which duty binds me to fulfil.
These airy kingdoms, and this wide command,
Are all the presents of your bounteous hand:
Yours is my sov'reign's grace; and, as your guest,
I sit with gods at their celestial feast;
Raise tempests at your pleasure, or subdue;
Dispose of empire, which I hold from you.'
He said, and hurl'd against the mountain side
His quiv'ring spear, and all the god applied.
The raging winds rush thro' the hollow wound,
And dance aloft in air, and skim along the ground;
Then, settling on the sea, the surges sweep,
Raise liquid mountains, and disclose the deep.
South, East, and West with mix'd confusion roar,
And roll the foaming billows to the shore.
The cables crack; the sailors' fearful cries
Ascend; and sable night involves the skies;
And heav'n itself is ravish'd from their eyes.
Loud peals of thunder from the poles ensue;
Then flashing fires the transient light renew;
The face of things a frightful image bears,
And present death in various forms appears.
Struck with unusual fright, the Trojan chief,
With lifted hands and eyes, invokes relief;
And, 'Thrice and four times happy those,' he cried,
'That under Ilian walls before their parents died!
Tydides, bravest of the Grecian train!
Why could not I by that strong arm be slain,
And lie by noble Hector on the plain,
Or great Sarpedon, in those bloody fields
Where Simois rolls the bodies and the shields
Of heroes, whose dismember'd hands yet bear
The dart aloft, and clench the pointed spear!'
Thus while the pious prince his fate bewails,
Fierce Boreas drove against his flying sails,
And rent the sheets; the raging billows rise,
And mount the tossing vessels to the skies:
Nor can the shiv'ring oars sustain the blow;
The galley gives her side, and turns her prow;
While those astern, descending down the steep,

Thro' gaping waves behold the boiling deep.
Three ships were hurried by the southern blast,
And on the secret shelves with fury cast.
Those hidden rocks th' Ausonian sailors knew:
They call'd them Altars, when they rose in view,
And show'd their spacious backs above the flood.
Three more fierce Eurus, in his angry mood,
Dash'd on the shallows of the moving sand,
And in mid ocean left them moor'd aland.
Orontes' bark, that bore the Lycian crew,
(A horrid sight!) ev'n in the hero's view,
From stem to stern by waves was overborne:
The trembling pilot, from his rudder torn,
Was headlong hurl'd; thrice round the ship was toss'd,
Then bulg'd at once, and in the deep was lost;
And here and there above the waves were seen
Arms, pictures, precious goods, and floating men.
The stoutest vessel to the storm gave way,
And suck'd thro' loosen'd planks the rushing sea.
Ilioneus was her chief: Alethes old,
Achates faithful, Abas young and bold,
Endur'd not less; their ships, with gaping seams,
Admit the deluge of the briny streams.
Meantime imperial Neptune heard the sound
Of raging billows breaking on the ground.
Displeas'd, and fearing for his wat'ry reign,
He rear'd his awful head above the main,
Serene in majesty; then roll'd his eyes
Around the space of earth, and seas, and skies.
He saw the Trojan fleet dispers'd, distress'd,
By stormy winds and wintry heav'n oppress'd.
Full well the god his sister's envy knew,
And what her aims and what her arts pursue.
He summon'd Eurus and the western blast,
And first an angry glance on both he cast;
Then thus rebuk'd: 'Audacious winds! from whence
This bold attempt, this rebel insolence?
Is it for you to ravage seas and land,
Unauthoriz'd by my supreme command?
To raise such mountains on the troubled main?

Whom I – but first 't is fit the billows to restrain;
And then you shall be taught obedience to my reign.
Hence! to your lord my royal mandate bear –
The realms of ocean and the fields of air
Are mine, not his. By fatal lot to me
The liquid empire fell, and trident of the sea.
His pow'r to hollow caverns is confin'd:
There let him reign, the jailer of the wind,
With hoarse commands his breathing subjects call,
And boast and bluster in his empty hall.'
He spoke; and, while he spoke, he smooth'd the sea,
Dispell'd the darkness, and restor'd the day.
Cymothoe, Triton, and the sea-green train
Of beauteous nymphs, the daughters of the main,
Clear from the rocks the vessels with their hands:
The god himself with ready trident stands,
And opes the deep, and spreads the moving sands;
Then heaves them off the shoals. Where'er he guides
His finny coursers and in triumph rides,
The waves unruffle and the sea subsides.
As, when in tumults rise th' ignoble crowd,
Mad are their motions, and their tongues are loud;
And stones and brands in rattling volleys fly,
And all the rustic arms that fury can supply:
If then some grave and pious man appear,
They hush their noise, and lend a list'ning ear;
He soothes with sober words their angry mood,
And quenches their innate desire of blood:
So, when the Father of the Flood appears,
And o'er the seas his sov'reign trident rears,
Their fury falls: he skims the liquid plains,
High on his chariot, and, with loosen'd reins,
Majestic moves along, and awful peace maintains.
The weary Trojans ply their shatter'd oars
To nearest land, and make the Libyan shores.
Within a long recess there lies a bay:
An island shades it from the rolling sea,
And forms a port secure for ships to ride;
Broke by the jutting land, on either side,

In double streams the briny waters glide.
Betwixt two rows of rocks a sylvan scene
Appears above, and groves for ever green:
A grot is form'd beneath, with mossy seats,
To rest the Nereids, and exclude the heats.
Down thro' the crannies of the living walls
The crystal streams descend in murm'ring falls:
No haulsers need to bind the vessels here,
Nor bearded anchors; for no storms they fear.
Sev'n ships within this happy harbor meet,
The thin remainders of the scatter'd fleet.
The Trojans, worn with toils, and spent with woes,
Leap on the welcome land, and seek their wish'd repose.
First, good Achates, with repeated strokes
Of clashing flints, their hidden fire provokes:
Short flame succeeds; a bed of wither'd leaves
The dying sparkles in their fall receives:
Caught into life, in fiery fumes they rise,
And, fed with stronger food, invade the skies.
The Trojans, dropping wet, or stand around
The cheerful blaze, or lie along the ground:
Some dry their corn, infected with the brine,
Then grind with marbles, and prepare to dine.
Aeneas climbs the mountain's airy brow,
And takes a prospect of the seas below,
If Capys thence, or Antheus he could spy,
Or see the streamers of Caicus fly.
No vessels were in view; but, on the plain,
Three beamy stags command a lordly train
Of branching heads: the more ignoble throng
Attend their stately steps, and slowly graze along.
He stood; and, while secure they fed below,
He took the quiver and the trusty bow
Achates us'd to bear: the leaders first
He laid along, and then the vulgar pierc'd;
Nor ceas'd his arrows, till the shady plain
Sev'n mighty bodies with their blood distain.
For the sev'n ships he made an equal share,
And to the port return'd, triumphant from the war.

The jars of gen'rous wine (Acestes' gift,
When his Trinacrian shores the navy left)
He sat abroach, and for the feast prepar'd,
In equal portions with the ven'son shar'd.
Thus while he dealt it round, the pious chief
With cheerful words allay'd the common grief:
'Endure, and conquer! Jove will soon dispose
To future good our past and present woes.
With me, the rocks of Scylla you have tried;
Th' inhuman Cyclops and his den defied.
What greater ills hereafter can you bear?
Resume your courage and dismiss your care,
An hour will come, with pleasure to relate
Your sorrows past, as benefits of Fate.
Thro' various hazards and events, we move
To Latium and the realms foredoom'd by Jove.
Call'd to the seat (the promise of the skies)
Where Trojan kingdoms once again may rise,
Endure the hardships of your present state;
Live, and reserve yourselves for better fate.'

## EZRA LOOMIS POUND

# The Seafarer

### (from the early Anglo-Saxon text)

May I for my own self song's truth reckon,
Journey's jargon, how I in harsh days
Hardship endured oft.
Bitter breast-cares have I abided,
Known on my keel many a care's hold,
And dire sea-surge, and there I oft spent
Narrow nightwatch nigh the ship's head
While she tossed close to cliffs. Coldly afflicted,

My feet were by frost benumbed.
Chill its chains are; chafing sighs
Hew my heart round and hunger begot
Mere-weary mood. Lest man know not
That he on dry land loveliest liveth,
List how I, care-wretched, on ice-cold sea,
Weathered the winter, wretched outcast
Deprived of my kinsmen;
Hung with hard ice-flakes, where hail-scur flew,
There I heard naught save the harsh sea
And ice-cold wave, at whiles the swan cries,
Did for my games the gannet's clamour,
Sea-fowls' loudness was for me laughter,
The mews' singing all my mead-drink.
Storms, on the stone-cliffs beaten, fell on the stern
In icy feathers; full oft the eagle screamed
With spray on his pinion.
　　　Not any protector
May make merry man faring needy.
This he little believes, who aye in winsome life
Abides 'mid burghers some heavy business,
Wealthy and wine-flushed, how I weary oft
Must bide above brine.
Neareth nightshade, snoweth from north,
Frost froze the land, hail fell on earth then
Corn of the coldest. Nathless there knocketh now
The heart's thought that I on high streams
The salt-wavy tumult traverse alone.
Moaneth alway my mind's lust
That I fare forth, that I afar hence
Seek out a foreign fastness.
For this there's no mood-lofty man over earth's midst,
Not though he be given his good, but will have in his youth
　　　greed;
Nor his deed to the daring, nor his king to the faithful
But shall have his sorrow for sea-fare
Whatever his lord will.
He hath not heart for harping, nor in ring-having
Nor winsomeness to wife, nor world's delight

Nor any whit else save the wave's slash,
Yet longing comes upon him to fare forth on the water.
Bosque taketh blossom, cometh beauty of berries,
Fields to fairness, land fares brisker,
All this admonisheth man eager of mood,
The heart turns to travel so that he then thinks
On flood-ways to be far departing.
Cuckoo calleth with gloomy crying,
He singeth summerward, bodeth sorrow,
The bitter heart's blood. Burgher knows not –
He the prosperous man – what some perform
Where wandering them widest draweth.
So that but now my heart burst from my breast-lock,
My mood 'mid the mere-flood,
Over the whale's acre, would wander wide.
On earth's shelter cometh oft to me,
Eager and ready, the crying lone-flyer,
Whets for the whale-path the heart irresistibly,
O'er tracks of ocean; seeing that anyhow
My lord deems to me this dead life
On loan and on land, I believe not
That any earth-weal eternal standeth
Save there be somewhat calamitous
That, ere a man's tide go, turn it to twain.
Disease or oldness or sword-hate
Beats out the breath from doom-gripped body.
And for this, every earl whatever, for those speaking after –
Laud of the living, boasteth some last word,
That he will work ere he pass onward,
Frame on the fair earth 'gainst foes his malice,
Daring ado, . . .
So that all men shall honour him after
And his laud beyond them remain 'mid the English,
Aye, for ever, a lasting life's-blast,
Delight mid the doughty
    Days little durable,
And all arrogance of earthen riches,
There come now no kings nor Caesars
Nor gold-giving lords like those gone.
Howe'er in mirth most magnified,

Whoe'er lived in life most lordliest,
Drear all this excellence, delights undurable!
Waneth the watch, but the world holdeth.
Tomb hideth trouble. The blade is layed low.
Earthly glory ageth and seareth.
No man at all going the earth's gait,
But age fares against him, his face paleth,
Grey-haired he groaneth, knows gone companions,
Lordly men are to earth o'ergiven,
Nor may he then the flesh-cover, whose life ceaseth,
Nor eat the sweet nor feel the sorry,
Nor stir hand nor think in mid heart,
And though he strew the grave with gold,
His born brothers, their buried bodies
Be an unlikely treasure hoard.

## GEOFFREY CHAUCER

# from The Canterbury Tales

### (from the General Prologue)

Whan that aprill with his shoures soote
The droghte of march hath perced to the roote,
And bathed every veyne in swich licour
Of which vertu engendred is the flour;
Whan zephirus eek with his sweete breeth
Inspired hath in every holt and heeth
Tendre croppes, and the yonge sonne
Hath in the ram his halve cours yronne,
And smale foweles maken melodye,
That slepen al the nyght with open ye
(so priketh hem nature in hir corages);
Thanne longen folk to goon on pilgrimages,
And palmeres for to seken straunge strondes,
To ferne halwes, kowthe in sondry londes;

And specially from every shires ende
Of engelond to caunterbury they wende,
The hooly blisful martir for to seke,
That hem hath holpen whan that they were seeke.

Bifil that in that season on a day,
In southwerk at the tabard as I lay
Redy to wenden on my pilgrymage
To caunterbury with ful devout corage,
At nyght was come into that hostelrye
Wel nyne and twenty in a compaignye,
Of sondry folk, by aventure yfalle
In felaweshipe, and pilgrimes were they alle,
That toward caunterbury wolden ryde.
The chambres and the stables weren wyde,
And wel we weren esed atte beste.
And shortly, whan the sonne was to reste,
So hadde I spoken with hem everichon
That I was of hir felaweshipe anon,
And made forward erly for to ryse,
To take oure wey ther as I yow devyse.

But nathelees, whil I have tyme and space,
Er that I ferther in this tale pace,
Me thynketh it acordaunt to resoun
To telle yow al the condicioun
Of ech of hem, so as it semed me,
And whiche they weren, and of what degree,
And eek in what array that they were inne;
And at a knyght than wol I first bigynne.

A knyght ther was, and that a worthy man,
That fro the tyme that he first bigan
To riden out, he loved chivalrie,
Trouthe and honour, fredom and curteisie.
Ful worthy was he in his lordes werre,
And therto hadde he riden, no man ferre,
As wel in cristendom as in hethenesse,
And evere honoured for his worthynesse.
At alisaundre he was whan it was wonne.

Ful ofte tyme he hadde the bord bigonne
Aboven alle nacions in pruce;
In lettow hadde he reysed and in ruce,
No cristen man so ofte of his degree.
In gernade at the seege eek hadde he be
Of algezir, and riden in belmarye.
At lyeys was he and at satalye,
Whan they were wonne; and in the grete see
At many a noble armee hadde he be.
At mortal batailles hadde he been fiftene,
And foughten for oure feith at tramyssene
In lystes thries, and ay slayn his foo.
This ilke worthy knyght hadde been also
Somtyme with the lord of palatye
Agayn another hethen in turkye.
And everemoore he hadde a sovereyn prys;
And though that he were worthy, he was wys,
And of his port as meeke as is a mayde.
He nevere yet no vileynye ne sayde
In al his lyf unto no maner wight.
He was a verray, parfit gentil knyght.
But, for to tellen yow of his array,
His hors were goode, but he was nat gay.
Of fustian he wered a gypon
Al bismotered with his habergeon,
For he was late ycome from his viage,
And wente for to doon his pilgrymage.
With hym ther was his sone, a yong squier,
A lovyere and a lusty bacheler,
With lokkes crulle as they were leyd in presse.
Of twenty yeer of age he was, I gesse.
Of his stature he was of evene lengthe,
And wonderly delyvere, and of greet strengthe.
And he hadde been somtyme in chyvachie
In flaundres, in artoys, and pycardie,
And born hym weel, as of so litel space,
In hope to stonden in his lady grace.
Embrouded was he, as it were a meede
Al ful of fresshe floures, whyte and reede.
Syngynge he was, or floytynge, al the day;

He was as fressh as is the month of may.
Short was his gowne, with sleves longe and wyde.
Wel koude he sitte on hors and faire ryde.
He koude songes make and wel endite,
Juste and eek daunce, and weel purtreye and write.
So hoote he lovede that by nyghtertale.
He sleep namoore than dooth a nyghtyngale.
Curteis he was, lowely, and servysable,
And carf biforn his fader at the table.
A yeman hadde he and servantz namo
At that tyme, for hym liste ride so,
And he was clad in cote and hood of grene.
A sheef of pecok arwes, bright and kene,
Under his belt he bar ful thriftily,
(wel koude he dresse his takel yemanly:
His arwes drouped noght with fetheres lowe)
And in his hand he baar a myghty bowe.
A not heed hadde he, with a broun visage.
Of wodecraft wel koude he al the usage.
Upon his arm he baar a gay bracer,
And by his syde a swerd and a bokeler,
And on that oother syde a gay daggere
Harneised wel and sharp as point of spere;
A cristopher on his brest of silver sheene.
An horn he bar, the bawdryk was of grene;
A forster was he, soothly, as I gesse.
Ther was also a nonne, a prioresse,
That of hir smylyng was ful symple and coy;
Hire gretteste ooth was but by seinte loy;
And she was cleped madame eglentyne.
Ful weel she soong the service dyvyne,
Entuned in hir nose ful semely,
And frenssh she spak ful faire and fetisly,
After the scole of stratford atte bowe,
For frenssh of parys was to hire unknowe.
At mete wel ytaught was she with alle:
She leet no morsel from hir lippes falle,
Ne wette hir fyngres in hir sauce depe;
Wel koude she carie a morsel and wel kepe
That no drope ne fille upon hire brest.

In curteisie was set ful muchel hir lest.
Hir over-lippe wyped she so clene
That in hir coppe ther was no ferthyng sene
Of grece, whan she dronken hadde hir draughte.
Ful semely after hir mete she raughte.
And sikerly she was of greet desport,
And ful plesaunt, and amyable of port,
And peyned hire to countrefete cheere
Of court, and to been estatlich of manere,
And to ben holden digne of reverence.
But, for to speken of hire conscience,
She was so charitable and so pitous
She wolde wepe, if that she saugh a mous
Kaught in a trappe, if it were deed or bledde.
Of smale houndes hadde she that she fedde
With rosted flessh, or milk and wastel-breed.
But soore wepte she if oon of hem were deed,
Or if men smoot it with a yerde smerte;
And al was conscience and tendre herte.
Ful semyly hir wympul pynched was,
Hir nose tretys, hir eyen greye as glas,
Hir mouth ful smal, and therto softe and reed;
But sikerly she hadde a fair forheed;
It was almoost a spanne brood, I trowe;
For, hardily, she was nat undergrowe.
Ful fetys was hir cloke, as I was war.
Of smal coral aboute hire arm she bar
A peire of bedes, gauded al with grene,
And theron heng a brooch of gold ful sheene,
On which ther was first write a crowned a,
And after amor vincit omnia.
Another nonne with hire hadde she,
That was hir chapeleyne, and preestes thre.
A monk ther was, a fair for the maistrie,
An outridere, that lovede venerie,
A manly man, to been an abbot able.
Ful many a deyntee hors hadde he in stable,
And whan he rood, men myghte his brydel heere
Gynglen in a whistlynge wynd als cleere
And eek as loude as dooth the chapel belle.

# SIR WALTER RALEGH

# The Passionate Man's Pilgrimage

Give me my scallop shell of quiet,
My staff of faith to walk upon,
My scrip of joy, immortal diet,
My bottle of salvation,
My gown of glory, hope's true gage,
And thus I'll take my pilgrimage.
Blood must be my body's balmer,
No other balm will there be given,
Whilst my soul, like a white palmer,
Travels to the land of heaven;
Over the silver mountains,
Where spring the nectar fountains;
And there I'll kiss
The bowl of bliss,
And drink my eternal fill
On every milken hill.
My soul will be a-dry before,
But after it will ne'er thirst more;
And by the happy blissful way
More peaceful pilgrims I shall see,
That have shook off their gowns of clay,
And go apparelled fresh like me.
I'll bring them first
To slake their thirst,
And then to taste those nectar suckets,
At the clear wells
Where sweetness dwells,
Drawn up by saints in crystal buckets.
And when our bottles and all we
Are fill'd with immortality,
Then the holy paths we'll travel,
Strew'd with rubies thick as gravel,

Ceilings of diamonds, sapphire floors,
High walls of coral, and pearl bowers.
  From thence to heaven's bribeless hall
Where no corrupted voices brawl,
No conscience molten into gold,
Nor forg'd accusers bought and sold,
No cause deferr'd, nor vain-spent journey,
For there Christ is the king's attorney,
Who pleads for all without degrees,
And he hath angels, but no fees.
When the grand twelve million jury
Of our sins and sinful fury,
'Gainst our souls black verdicts give,
Christ pleads his death, and then we live.
Be thou my speaker, taintless pleader,
Unblotted lawyer, true proceeder,
Thou movest salvation even for alms,
Not with a bribed lawyer's palms.
And this is my eternal plea
To him that made heaven, earth, and sea,
Seeing my flesh must die so soon,
And want a head to dine next noon,
Just at the stroke when my veins start and spread,
Set on my soul an everlasting head.
Then am I ready, like a palmer fit,
To tread those blest paths which before I writ.


## MICHAEL DRAYTON

# To the Virginian Voyage

You brave heroic minds
  Worthy your country's name,
    That honour still pursue;
    Go and subdue!

Whilst loitering hinds
  Lurk here at home with shame.

Britons, you stay too long:
  Quickly aboard bestow you,
    And with a merry gale
    Swell your stretch'd sail
With vows as strong
  As the winds that blow you.

Your course securely steer,
  West and by south forth keep!
    Rocks, lee-shores, nor shoals
    When Eolus scowls
You need not fear;
  So absolute the deep.

And cheerfully at sea
  Success you still entice
    To get the pearl and gold,
    And ours to hold
Virginia,
  Earth's only paradise.

Where nature hath in store
  Fowl, venison, and fish,
    And the fruitfull'st soil
    Without your toil
Three harvests more,
  All greater than your wish.

And the ambitious vine
  Crowns with his purple mass
    The cedar reaching high
    To kiss the sky,
The cypress, pine,
  And useful sassafras.

To whom the Golden Age
  Still nature's laws doth give,
    No other cares attend,

But them to defend
From winter's rage,
  That long there doth not live.

When as the luscious smell
  Of that delicious land
    Above the seas that flows
    The clear wind throws,
Your hearts to swell
  Approaching the dear strand;

In kenning of the shore
  (Thanks to God first given)
    O you the happiest men,
    Be frolic then!
Let cannons roar,
  Frighting the wide heaven.

And in regions far,
  Such heroes bring ye forth
    As those from whom we came;
    And plant our name
Under that star
  Not known unto our North.

And as there plenty grows
  Of laurel everywhere –
    Apollo's sacred tree –
    You it may see
A poet's brows
  To crown, that may sing there.

Thy voyages attend,
  Industrious Hakluyt,
    Whose reading shall inflame
    Men to seek fame,
And much commend
  To after times thy wit.

## JOHN DONNE

# The Sun Rising

Busy old fool, unruly Sun,
Why dost thou thus,
Through windows, and through curtains, call on us?
Must to thy motions lovers' seasons run?
Saucy pedantic wretch, go chide
Late schoolboys, and sour prentices,
Go tell court-huntsmen that the king will ride,
Call country ants to harvest offices,
Love, all alike, no season knows, nor clime,
Nor hours, days, months, which are the rags of time.

Thy beams, so reverend and strong
Why shouldst thou think?
I could eclipse and cloud them with a wink,
But that I would not lose her sight so long:
If her eyes have not blinded thine,
Look, and tomorrow late, tell me
Whether both th'Indias of spice and mine
Be where thou leftst them, or lie here with me.
Ask for those kings whom thou saw'st yesterday,
And thou shalt hear: 'All here in one bed lay.'

She's all states, and all princes I,
Nothing else is.
Princes do but play us; compar'd to this,
All honour's mimic, all wealth alchemy.
Thou, sun, art half as happy'as we,
In that the world's contracted thus;
Thine age asks ease, and since thy duties be
To warm the world, that's done in warming us.
Shine here to us, and thou art everywhere;
This bed thy centre is, these walls, thy sphere.

## JOHN DONNE

# To Sir H. W. at His Going Ambassador to Venice

After those reverend papers, whose soule is
  Our good and great Kings lov'd hand and fear'd name,
By which to you he derives much of his,
  And (how he may) makes you almost the same,

A Taper of his Torch, a copie writ
  From his Originall, and a faire beame
Of the same warme, and dazeling Sun, though it
  Must in another Sphere his vertue streame:

After those learned papers which your hand
  Hath stor'd with notes of use and pleasure too,
From which rich treasury you may command
  Fit matter whether you will write or doe:

After those loving papers, where friends send
  With glad griefe, to your Sea-ward steps, farewel,
Which thicken on you now, as prayers ascend
  To heaven in troupes at'a good man's passing bell:

Admit this honest paper, and allow
  It such an audience as your selfe would aske;
What you must say at Venice this meanes now,
  And hath for nature, what you have for taske:

To sweare much love, not to be chang'd before
  Honour alone will to your fortune fit;
Nor shall I then honour your fortune, more
  Then I have done your honour wanting it.

But 'tis an easier load (though both oppresse)
  To want, then governe greatnesse, for wee are
In that, our owne and onely businesse,
  In this, wee must for others vices care;

'Tis therefore well your spirits now are plac'd
  In their last Furnace, in activity;
Which fits them (Schooles and Courts and Warres o'rpast)
  To touch and test in any best degree.

For mee, (if there be such a thing as I)
  Fortune (if there be such a thing as shee)
Spies that I beare so well her tyranny,
  That she thinks nothing else so fit for mee;

But though she part us, to heare my oft prayers
  For your increase, God is as neere mee here;
And to send you what I shall begge, his staires
  In length and ease are alike every where.

## GEORGE TURBEVILLE

# To Spencer

If I should now forget, or not remember thee,
Thou, Spencer, might'st a foul rebuke and shame impute to
  me.
For I to open show did love thee passing well,
And thou wert he at parture whom I loathed to bid farewell.
And as I went thy friend, so I continue still:
No better proof thou canst than this desire of true good will.
I do remember well when needs I should away,
And that the post would license us no longer time to stay:
Thou wrungst me by the fist, and holding fast my hand,
Didst crave of me to send thee news, and how I liked the
  land.
It is a sandy soil, no very fruitful vein,
More waste and woody grounds there are than closes fit for
  grain.

Yet grain there growing is, which they untimely take,
And cut or e'er the corn be ripe; they mow it on a stake.
And laying sheaf by sheaf, their harvest so they dry,
They make the greater haste, for fear the frost the corn
    destroy.
For in the winter time, so glary is the ground,
As neither grass, nor other grain, in pastures may be found.
In comes the cattle then, the sheep, the colt, the cow,
Fast by his bed the mousik then a lodging doth allow,
Whom he with fodder feeds, and holds as dear as life:
And thus they wear the winter with the mousik and his wife.
Seven months the winter dures, the glare it is so great,
As it is May before he turn his ground to sow his wheat.
The bodies eke that die unburied lie they then,
Laid up in coffins made of fir, as well the poorest men
As those of greater state: the cause is lightly found,
For that in winter time they cannot come to break the
    ground.
And wood so plenteous is, quite throughout all the land,
As rich and poor, at time of death assured of coffins stand.
Perhaps thou musest much, how this may stand with reason,
That bodies dead can uncorrupt abide so long a season.
Take this for certain troth, as soon as the heat is gone,
The force of cold the body binds as hard as any stone,
Without offence at all to any living thing:
As so they lie in perfect state, till next return of spring.
Their beasts be like to ours, as far as I can see,
For shape, and show, but somewhat less of bulk and bone
    they be.
Of wat'rish taste, the flesh not firm, like English beef,
And yet it serves them very well, and is a good relief.
Their sheep are very small, sharp-cingled, handful long;
Great store of fowl on sea and land, moorish reeds among.
The greatness of the store doth make the prices less;
Besides in all the land they know not how good meat to
    dress.
They use neither broach nor spit, but when the stove they
    heat
They put their victuals in a pan, and so they bake their meat.
No pewter to be had, no dishes but of wood,

No use of trenchers, cups cut out of birch are very good.
They use but wooden spoons, which hanging in a case
Each mousik at his girdle ties, and he thinks it no disgrace.
With whittles two or three, the better man the moe,
The chiefest Russies in the land with spoon and knives do go.
Their houses are not huge of building, but they say,
They plant them in the loftiest ground, to shift the snow
   away,
Which in the winter time each where full thick doth lie:
Which makes them have the more desire, to set their houses
   high.
No stone work is in use, their roofs of rafters be,
One linked in another fast, their walls are all of tree.
Of masts both long, and large, with moss put in between,
To keep the force of weather out – I never erst have seen
A gross device so good – and on the roof they lay
The burthern bark, to rid the rain and sudden showers away.
In every room a stove, to serve the winter turn;
Of wood they have sufficient store, as much as they can burn.
They have no English glass; of slices of a rock
Hight sluda they their windows make, that English glass doth
   mock.
They cut it very thin, and sew it with a thread
In pretty order like to panes, to serve their present need.
No other glass, good faith, doth give a better light:
And sure the rock is nothing rich, the cost is very slight.
The chiefest place is that, where hangs the god by it,
The owner of the house himself doth never sit,
Unless his better come, to whom he yields the seat:
The stranger bending to the god, the ground with brow must
   beat.
And in that very place which they most sacred deem,
The stranger lies: a token that his guest he doth esteem.
Where he is wont to have a bear's skin for his bed,
And must, instead of pillow, clap his saddle to his head.
In Russia other shift there is not to be had,
For where the bedding is not good, the bolsters are but bad.
I mused very much, what made them so to lie,
Sith in their country down is rife, and feathers out of cry:
Unless it be because the country is so hard,

They fear by niceness of a bed their bodies would be marred.
I wished thee oft with us, save that I stood in fear
Thou wouldst have loathed to have laid thy limbs upon a
    bear,
As I and Stafford did, that was my mate in bed:
And yet (we thank the God of heaven) we both right well and
    sped.
Lo thus I make an end: none other news to thee,
But that the country is too cold, the people beastly be.
I write not all I know, but I touch but here and there,
For if I should, my pen would pinch, and eke offend I fear.
Whoso shall read this verse, conjecture of the rest,
And think by reason of our trade, that I do think the best.
But if no traffic were, then could I boldly pen
The hardness of the soil, and eke the manners of the men.
They say the lion's paw gives judgment of the beast:
And so may you deem of the great, by reading of the least.

## ANDREW MARVELL

# Song of the Emigrants in Bermuda

Where the remote Bermudas ride
In the ocean's bosom unespied,
From a small boat that row'd along
The listening winds received this song: –
    'What should we do but sing His praise
That led us through the watery maze
Where He the huge sea-monsters wracks,
That lift the deep upon their backs,
Unto an isle so long unknown,
And yet far kinder than our own?
He lands us on a grassy stage,
Safe from the storms, and prelate's rage
He gave us this eternal Spring

Which here enamels everything,
And sends the fowls to us in care
On daily visits through the air.
He hangs in shades the orange bright
Like golden lamps in a green night,
And does in the pomegranates close
Jewels more rich than Ormus shows;
He makes the figs our mouths to meet
And throws the melons at our feet;
But apples plants of such a price,
No tree could ever bear them twice.
With cedars chosen by His hand
From Lebanon He stores the land;
And makes the hollow seas that roar
Proclaim the ambergris on shore.
He cast (of which we rather boast)
The Gospel's pearl upon our coast;
And in these rocks for us did frame
A temple where to sound His name.
O let our voice His praise exalt
Till it arrive at Heaven's vault,
Which then perhaps rebounding may
Echo beyond the Mexique bay!'
    Thus sang they in the English boat
A holy and a cheerful note:
And all the way, to guide their chime,
With falling oars they kept the time.

## MRS ANNE KILLIGREW

# On a Young Lady
# Whose Lord was Travelling

On a young Lady
Whose LORD was Travelling.
NO sooner I pronounced Celinda's name,
But Troops of wing'd Pow'rs did chant the fame:
Not those the Poet's Bows and Arrows lend,
But such as on the Altar do attend.
Celinda nam'd, Flow'rs spring up from the Ground,
Excited meerly with the Charming Sound.
Celinda, the Court's Glory, and its fear,
The gaz'd at Wonder, where she does appear.
Celinda great in Birth, greater in Meen,
Yet none so humble as this Fair-One's seen.
Her Youth and Beauty justly might disdain,
But the least Pride her Glories ne're did stain.

Celinda of each State th'ambitious Strife,
At once a Noble Virgin, and a Wife
Who, while her Gallant Lord in Forraign parts
Adorns his Youth with all accomplisht Arts,
Grows ripe at home in Vertue, more than Years,
And in each Grace a Miracle appears!
When other of her Age a madding go,
To th' Park and Plays, and ev'ry publick Show,
Proud from their Parents Bondage they have broke,
Though justly freed, she still does wear the Yoke;
Preferring more her Mothers Friend to be,
Than Idol of the Town's Loose-Gallantry.
On her she to the Temple does attend,
Where they their Blessed Hours both save and spend.
They Smile, they Joy, together they do Pray,
You'd think two Bodies did One Soul obey:
Like Angels thus they do reflect their Bliss,
And their bright Vertues each the other kiss.

Return young Lord, while thou abroad dost rome
The World to see, thou loosest Heaven at Home.


## WILLIAM COWPER

# The Solitude of Alexander Selkirk

I am monarch of all I survey;
My right there is none to dispute;
From the centre all round to the sea
I am lord of the fowl and the brute
O Solitude! where are the charms
That sages have seen in thy face?
Better dwell in the midst of alarms,
Than reign in this horrible place.

I am out of humanity's reach;
I must finish my journey alone;
Never hear the sweet music of speech –
I start at the sound of my own;
The beasts that roam over the plain
My form with indifference see –
They are so unacquainted with man,
Their tameness is shocking to me.

Society, Friendship, and Love
Divinely bestow'd upon man,
Oh had I the wings of a dove
How soon would I taste you again!
My sorrows I then might assuage
In the ways of religion and truth,
Might learn from the wisdom of age,
And be cheer'd by the sallies of youth.

Ye winds that have made me your sport,
Convey to this desolate shore
Some cordial endearing report
Of a land I shall visit no more.
My friends, do they now and then send
A wish or a thought after me?
O tell me I yet have a friend,
Though a friend I am never to see.

How fleet is a glance of the mind!
Compared with the speed of its flight,
The tempest itself lags behind,
And the swift-wingèd arrows of light.
When I think of my own native land,
In a moment I seem to be there;
But, alas! recollection at hand
Soon hurries me back to despair.

But the sea-fowl is gone to her nest,
The beast is laid down in his lair;
Even here is a season of rest,
And I to my cabin repair.
There's mercy in every place;
And mercy – encouraging thought! –
Gives even affliction a grace,
And reconciles man to his lot.

## LADY MARY WORTLEY MONTAGU

# Written in the Chiosk of the British Palace, at Pera, Overlooking the City of Constantinople, Dec. 26, 1718 [1717]

Give me, great God! said I, a little farm,
In summer shady, and in winter warm;
Where a clear spring gives birth to murm'ring brooks,
By nature gliding down the mossy rocks.
Not artfully by leaden pipes convey'd,
Or greatly falling in a forc'd cascade,
Pure and unsullied winding through the shade.
All bounteous Heaven has added to my prayer,
A softer climate and a purer air.
Our frozen Isle now chilling winter binds,
Deform'd by rains, and rough with blasting winds;
The wither'd woods grow white with hoary frost,
By driving storms their verdant beauty lost;
The trembling birds their leafless covert shun,
And seek in distant climes a warmer sun:
The water-nymphs their silent urns deplore,
Ev'n Thames, benumb'd, 's a river now no more:
The barren meads no longer yield delight,
By glist'ning snows made painful to the sight.
Here summer reigns with one eternal smile,
Succeeding harvests bless the happy soil;
Fair fertile fields, to whom indulgent Heaven
Has ev'ry charm of ev'ry season given.
No killing cold deforms the beauteous year,
The springing flowers no coming winter fear.
But as the parent rose decays and dies,
The infant buds with brighter colours rise,
And with fresh sweets the mother's scent supplies.
Near them the violet grows with odours blest,
And blooms in more than Tyrian purple drest;
The rich jonquils their golden beams display,

And shine in glory's emulating day;
The peaceful groves their verdant leaves retain,
The streams still murmur undefil'd with rain,
And tow'ring greens adorn the fruitful plain.
The warbling kind uninterrupted sing,
Warm'd with enjoyments of perpetual spring.
Here, at my window, I at once survey
The crowded city and resounding sea;
In distant views the Asian mountains rise,
And lose their snowy summits in the skies;
Above these mountains proud Olympus tow'rs,
The parliamental seat of heavenly pow'rs!
New to the sight my ravish'd eyes admire
Each gilded crescent and each antique spire,
The marble mosques, beneath whose ample domes
Fierce warlike sultans sleep in peaceful tombs;
Those lofty structures, once the Christian's boast,
Their names, their beauty, and their honours lost;
Those altars bright with gold and sculpture grac'd,
By barb'rous zeal of savage foes defac'd;
Soph'a alone, her ancient name retains,
Though th' unbeliever now her shrine profanes;
Where holy saints have died in sacred cells,
Where monarchs pray'd, the frantic dervise dwells.
How art thou fall'n, imperial city, low!
Where are thy hopes of Roman glory now?
Where are thy palaces by prelates rais'd?
Where Grecian artists all their skill display'd,
Before the happy sciences decay'd;
So vast, that youthful kings might here reside,
So splendid, to content a patriarch's pride;
Convents where emperors profess'd of old,
The labour'd pillars that their triumphs told;
Vain monuments of them that once were great,
Sunk undistinguis'd by one common fate;
One little spot the tenure small contains,
Of Greek nobility the poor remains;
Where other Helens, with like powerful charms,
Had once engag'd the warring world in arms;
Those names which royal ancestors can boast,

In mean mechanic arts obscurely lost;
Those eyes a second Homer might inspire,
Fix'd at the loom, destroy their useless fire:
Griev'd at a view, which struck upon my mind
The short-liv'd vanity of humankind.
In gaudy objects I indulge my sight,
And turn where Eastern pomp gives gay delight;
See the vast train in various habits drest,
By the bright scimitar and sable vest
The proud vizier distinguish'd o'er the rest!
Six slaves in gay attire his bridle hold,
His bridle rich with gems, and stirrups gold;
His snowy steed adorn'd with costly pride,
Whole troops of soldiers mounted by his side,
These top the plumy crest Arabian coursers guide.
With artful duty all decline their eyes,
No bellowing shouts of noisy crowds arise;
Silence, in solemn state, the march attends,
Till at the dread divan the slow procession ends.
Yet not these prospects all profusely gay,
The gilded navy that adorns the sea,
The rising city in confusion fair,
Magnificently form'd, irregular,
Where woods and palaces at once surprise,
Gardens on gardens, domes on domes arise,
And endless beauties tire the wand'ring eyes,
So soothe my wishes, or so charm my mind,
As this retreat secure from humankind.
No knave's successful craft does spleen excite,
No coxcomb's tawdry splendour shocks my sight,
No mob-alarm awakes my female fear,
No praise my mind, nor envy hurts my ear,
Ev'n fame itself can hardly reach me here;
Impertinence, with all her tattling train,
Fair-sounding flattery's delicious bane;
Censorious folly, noisy party rage,
The thousand tongues with which she must engage
Who dare have virtue in a vicious age.

## MARY ROBINSON

# Stanzas Written Between Dover and Calais, July 20, 1792

Bounding billow, cease thy motion,
Bear me not so swiftly o'er;
Cease thy roaring, foamy ocean,
I will tempt thy rage no more.

Ah! within my bosom beating,
Varying passions wildly reign;
Love, with proud Resentment meeting,
Throbs by turns, of joy and pain.

Joy, that far from foes I wander,
Where their taunts can reach no more;
Pain, that woman's heart grows fonder
When her dream of bliss is o'er!

Love, by fickle fancy banish'd,
Spurn'd by hope, indignant flies;
Yet when love and hope are vanish'd,
Restless mem'ry never dies.

Far I go, where fate shall lead me,
Far across the troubled deep;
Where no stranger's ear shall heed me,
Where no eye for me shall weep.

Proud has been my fatal passion!
Proud my injured heart shall be!
While each thought, each inclination,
Still shall prove me worthy thee!

Not one sigh shall tell my story;
Not one tear my cheek shall stain;
Silent grief shall be my glory, –
Grief, that stoops not to complain!

Let the bosom prone to ranging,
Still by ranging seek a cure;
Mine disdains the thought of changing,
Proudly destin'd to endure.

Yet, ere far from all I treasur'd,
– ere I bid adieu;
Ere my days of pain are measur'd,
Take the song that's still thy due!

Yet, believe, no servile passions
Seek to charm thy vagrant mind;
Well I know thy inclinations,
Wav'ring as the passing wind.

I have lov'd thee, – dearly lov'd thee,
Through an age of worldly woe;
How ungrateful I have prov'd thee
Let my mournful exile show!

Ten long years of anxious sorrow,
Hour by hour I counted o'er;
Looking forward, till to-morrow,
Every day I lov'd thee more!

Pow'r and splendour could not charm me;
I no joy in wealth could see!
Nor could threats or fears alarm me,
Save the fear of losing thee!

When the storms of fortune press'd thee,
I have wept to see thee weep!
When relentless cares distress'd thee,
I have lull'd those cares to sleep!

When with thee, what ills could harm me?
Thou couldst every pang assuage;
But when absent, nought could charm me;
Every moment seem'd an age.

Fare thee well, ungrateful rover!
Welcome Gallia's hostile shore:
Now the breezes waft me over;
Now we part – TO MEET NO MORE.

## CHARLOTTE SMITH

# from Beachy Head 1807 [comp. 1806] Cliffs in South-East England

On thy stupendous summit, rock sublime!
That o'er the channel rear'd, half way at sea
The mariner at early morning hails,
I would recline; while Fancy should go forth,
And represent the strange and awful hour
Of vast concussion; when the Omnipotent
Stretch'd forth his arm, and rent the solid hills,
Bidding the impetuous main flood rush between
The rifted shores, and from the continent
Eternally divided this green isle.
Imperial lord of the high southern coast!
From thy projecting head-land I would mark
Far in the east the shades of night disperse,
Melting and thinned, as from the dark blue wave
Emerging, brilliant rays of arrowy light
Dart from the horizon; when the glorious sun
Just lifts above it his resplendent orb.
Advances now, with feathery silver touched,
The rippling tide of flood; glisten the sands,
While, inmates of the chalky clefts that scar
Thy sides precipitous, with shrill harsh cry,
Their white wings glancing in the level beam,
The terns, and gulls, and tarrocks, seek their food,
And thy rough hollows echo to the voice
Of the gray choughs, and ever restless daws,

With clamour, not unlike the chiding hounds,
While the lone shepherd, and his baying dog,
Drive to thy turfy crest his bleating flock.

The high meridian of the day is past,
And Ocean now, reflecting the calm Heaven,
Is of cerulean hue; and murmurs low
The tide of ebb, upon the level sands.
The sloop, her angular canvas shifting still,
Catches the light and variable airs
That but a little crisp the summer sea.
Dimpling its tranquil surface.
                    Afar off,
And just emerging from the arch immense
Where seem to part the elements, a fleet
Of fishing vessels stretch their lesser sails;
While more remote, and like a dubious spot
Just hanging in the horizon, laden deep,
The ship of commerce richly freighted, makes
Her slower progress, on her distant voyage,
Bound to the orient climates, where the sun
Matures the spice within its odorous shell,
And, rivalling the gray worm's filmy toil,
Bursts from its pod the vegetable down;
Which in long turban'd wreaths, from torrid heat
Defends the brows of Asia's countless casts.
There the Earth hides within her glowing breast
The beamy adamant, and the round pearl
Enchased in rugged covering; which the slave,
With perilous and breathless toil, tears off
From the rough sea-rock, deep beneath the waves.
These are the toys of Nature; and her sport
Of little estimate in Reason's eye:
And they who reason, with abhorrence see
Man, for such gaudes and baubles, violate
The sacred freedom of his fellow man –
Erroneous estimate! As Heaven's pure air,
Fresh as it blows on this airial height,
Or sound of seas upon the stony strand,
Or inland, the gay harmony of birds,

And winds that wander in the leafy woods;
Are to the unadulterate taste more worth
Than the elaborate harmony, brought out
From fretted stop, or modulated airs
Of vocal science. – So the brightest gems,
Glancing resplendent on the regal crown,
Or trembling in the high born beauty's ear,
Are poor and paltry, to the lovely light
Of the fair star, that as the day declines,
Attendant on her queen, the crescent moon,
Bathes her bright tresses in the eastern wave.
For now the sun is verging to the sea,
And as he westward sinks, the floating clouds
Suspended, move upon the evening gale,
And gathering round his orb, as if to shade
The insufferable brightness, they resign
Their gauzy whiteness; and more warm'd, assume
All hues of purple. There, transparent gold
Mingles with ruby tints, and sapphire gleams,
And colours, such as Nature through her works
Shews only in the ethereal canopy.
Thither aspiring Fancy fondly soars,
Wandering sublime thro' visionary vales,
Where bright pavilions rise, and trophies, fann'd
By airs celestial; and adorn'd with wreaths
Of flowers that bloom amid elysian bowers.
Now bright, and brighter still the colours glow,
Till half the lustrous orb within the flood
Seems to retire: the flood reflecting still
Its splendor, and in mimic glory drest;
Till the last ray shot upward, fires the clouds
With blazing crimson; then in paler light,
Long lines of tenderer radiance, lingering yield
To partial darkness; and on the opposing side
The early moon distinctly rising, throws
Her pearly brilliance on the trembling tide.

The fishermen, who at set seasons pass
Many a league off at sea their toiling night,
Now hail their comrades, from their daily task

Returning; and make ready for their own,
With the night tide commencing: – The night tide
Bears a dark vessel on, whose hull and sails
Mark her a coaster from the north. Her keel
Now ploughs the sand; and sidelong now she leans,
While with loud clamours her athletic crew
Unload her; and resounds the busy hum
Along the wave-worn rocks. Yet more remote,
Where the rough cliff hangs beetling o'er its base,
All breathes repose; the water's rippling sound
Scarce heard; but now and then the sea-snipe's cry
Just tells that something living is abroad;
And sometimes crossing on the moonbright line,
Glimmers the skiff, faintly discern'd awhile,
Then lost in shadow.
             Contemplation here,
High on her throne of rock, aloof may sit,
And bid recording Memory unfold
Her scroll voluminous – bid her retrace
The period, when from Neustria's hostile shore
The Norman launch'd his galleys, and the bay
O'er which that mass of ruin frowns even now
In vain and sullen menace, then received
The new invaders; a proud martial race,
Of Scandinavia the undaunted sons,
Whom Dogon, Fier-a-bras, and Humfroi led
To conquest: while Trinacria to their power
Yielded her wheaten garland; and when thou,
Parthenope! within thy fertile bay
Receiv'd the victors –
            In the mailed ranks

Pevensey Castle
Of Normans landing on the British coast
Rode Taillefer; and with astounding voice
Thunder'd the war song daring Roland sang
First in the fierce contention: vainly brave,
One not inglorious struggle England made –
But failing, saw the Saxon heptarchy
Finish for ever. – Then the holy pile,

Yet seen upon the field of conquest, rose,
Where to appease heaven's wrath for so much blood,
The conqueror bade unceasing prayers ascend,
And requiems for the slayers and the slain.
But let not modern Gallia form from hence
Presumptuous hopes, that ever thou again,
Queen of the isles! shalt crouch to foreign arms.
The enervate sons of Italy may yield;
And the Iberian, all his trophies torn
And wrapp'd in Superstition's monkish weed,
May shelter his abasement, and put on
Degrading fetters. Never, never thou!
Imperial mistress of the obedient sea;
But thou, in thy integrity secure,
Shalt now undaunted meet a world in arms.


## SAMUEL TAYLOR COLERIDGE

# Kubla Khan
# Or, a Vision in a Dream. A Fragment

In Xanadu did Kubla Khan
A stately pleasure-dome decree:
Where Alph, the sacred river, ran
Through caverns measureless to man

Down to a sunless sea.

So twice five miles of fertile ground
With walls and towers were girdled round:
And there were gardens bright with sinuous rills,
Where blossomed many an incense-bearing tree;
And here were forests ancient as the hills,
Enfolding sunny spots of greenery.

But oh! that deep romantic chasm which slanted
Down the green hill athwart a cedarn cover!
A savage place! as holy and enchanted
As e'er beneath a waning moon was haunted
By woman wailing for her demon-lover!
And from this chasm, with ceaseless turmoil seething,
As if this earth in fast thick pants were breathing,
A mighty fountain momently was forced:
Amid whose swift half-intermitted burst
Huge fragments vaulted like rebounding hail,
Or chaffy grain beneath the thresher's flail:
And 'mid these dancing rocks at once and ever
It flung up momently the sacred river.
Five miles meandering with a mazy motion
Through wood and dale the sacred river ran,
Then reached the caverns measureless to man,
And sank in tumult to a lifeless ocean:
And 'mid this tumult Kubla heard from far
Ancestral voices prophesying war!

The shadow of the dome of pleasure
Floated midway on the waves;
Where was heard the mingled measure
From the fountain and the caves.

It was a miracle of rare device,
A sunny pleasure-dome with caves of ice!

A damsel with a dulcimer
In a vision once I saw:
It was an Abyssinian maid,
And on her dulcimer she played,
Singing of Mount Abora.
Could I revive within me
Her symphony and song,
To such a deep delight 'twould win me,

That with music loud and long,
I would build that dome in air,

That sunny dome! those caves of ice!
And all who heard should see them there,
And all should cry, Beware! Beware!
His flashing eyes, his floating hair!
Weave a circle round him thrice,
And close your eyes with holy dread,
For he on honey-dew hath fed,
And drunk the milk of Paradise.


# SAMUEL TAYLOR COLERIDGE

## France: An Ode

[1]
Ye Clouds! that far above me float and pause,
  Whose pathless march no mortal may control!
Ye Ocean-Waves! that, wheresoe'er ye roll,
Yield homage only to eternal laws!
Ye Woods! that listen to the night-birds singing,
  Midway the smooth and perilous slope reclined.
Save when your own imperious branches swinging,
  Have made a solemn music of the wind!
Where, like a man beloved of God,
Through glooms, which never woodman trod,
    How oft, pursuing fancies holy,
My moonlight way o'er flowering weeds I wound,
    Inspired, beyond the guess of folly,
By each rude shape and wild unconquerable sound!
O ye loud Waves! and O ye Forests high!
    And O ye Clouds that far above me soared!
Thou rising Sun! thou blue rejoicing Sky!
    Yea, every thing that is and will be free!
    Bear witness for me, wheresoe'er ye be,
    With what deep worship I have still adored
    The spirit of divinest Liberty.

[2]

When France in wrath her giant-limbs upreared,
  And with that oath, which smote air, earth, and sea,
  Stamped her strong foot and said she would be free,
Bear witness for me, how I hoped and feared!
With what a joy my lofty gratulation
  Unawed I sang, amid a slavish band:
And when to whelm the disenchanted nation,
  Like fiends embattled by a wizard's wand,
    The Monarchs marched in evil day,
    And Britain joined the dire array;
  Though dear her shores and circling ocean,
Though many friendships, many youthful loves
  Had swoln the patriot emotion
And flung a magic light o'er all her hills and groves;
Yet still my voice, unaltered, sang defeat
  To all that braved the tyrant-quelling lance,
And shame too long delayed and vain retreat!
For n'er, O Liberty! with partial aim
I dimmed thy light or damped thy holy flame;
  But blessed the paeans of delivered France,
And hung my head and wept at Britain's name.


[3]

'And what,' I said, 'though Blasphemy's loud scream
  With that sweet music of deliverance strove!
  Though all the fierce and drunken passions wove
A dance more wild than e'er was maniac's dream!
  Ye storms, that round the dawning East assembled,
The Sun was rising, though ye hid his light!'
  And when, to soothe my soul, that hoped and trembled,
The dissonance ceased, and all seemed calm and bright;
  When France her front deep-scarr'd and gory
  Concealed with clustering wreaths of glory;
    When, insupportably advancing,
  Her arm made mockery of the warrior's ramp;
    While timid looks of fury glancing,
  Domestic treason, crushed beneath her fatal stamp,
Writhed like a wounded dragon in his gore;
  Then I reproached my fears that would not flee;

'And soon,' I said, 'shall Wisdom teach her lore
In the low huts of them that toil and groan!
And, conquering by her happiness alone,
  Shall France compel the nations to be free,
Till Love and Joy look round, and call the Earth their own.'

[4]

Forgive me, Freedom! O forgive those dreams!
  I hear thy voice, I hear thy loud lament,
  From bleak Helvetia's icy caverns sent –
I hear thy groans upon her blood-stained streams!
  Heroes, that for your peaceful country perished,
  And ye that, fleeing, spot your mountain-snows
  With bleeding wounds; forgive me, that I cherished
One thought that ever blessed your cruel foes!
  To scatter rage, and traitorous guilt,
  Where Peace her jealous home had built;
  A patriot-race to disinherit
Of all that made their stormy wilds so dear;
  And with inexpiable spirit
To taint the bloodless freedom of the mountaineer –
O France, that mockest Heaven, adulterous, blind,
  And patriot only in pernicious toils!
Are these thy boasts, Champion of human kind?
  To mix with Kings in the low lust of sway,
Yell in the hunt, and share the murderous prey;
To insult the shrine of Liberty with spoils
  From freemen torn; to tempt and to betray?

[5]

The Sensual and the Dark rebel in vain,
Slaves by their own compulsion! In mad game
They burst their manacles and wear the name
  Of Freedom, graven on a heavier chain!
O Liberty! with profitless endeavour
Have I pursued thee, many a weary hour;
  But thou nor swell'st the victor's strain, nor ever
Didst breathe thy soul in forms of human power.
  Alike from all, howe'er they praise thee,
  (Nor prayer, nor boastful name delays thee)

Alike from Priestcraft's harpy minions,
  And factious Blasphemy's obscener slaves,
    Thou speedest on thy subtle pinions,
The guide of homeless winds, and playmate of the waves!
And there I felt thee! – on that sea-cliff's verge,
    Whose pines, scarce travelled by the breeze above,
Had made one murmur with the distant surge!
Yes, while I stood and gazed, my temples bare,
And shot my being through earth, sea, and air,
    Possessing all things with intensest love,
      O Liberty! my spirit felt thee there.

## WILLIAM WORDSWORTH

# Admonition to a Traveller

Yes, there is holy pleasure in thine eye!
  The lovely cottage in the guardian nook
  Hath stirr'd thee deeply; with its own dear brook,
Its own small pasture, almost its own sky!
But covet not the abode; O do not sigh
  As many do, repining while they look –
  Intruders, who would tear from Nature's book
This precious leaf with harsh impiety.
Think what the home would be if it were thine,
  Even thine, though few thy wants! – Roof, window, door,
  The very flowers are sacred to the Poor,
The roses to the porch which they entwine:
Yea, all that now enchants thee, from the day
On which it should be touch'd, would melt away!

## WILLIAM WORDSWORTH
# England and Switzerland, 1802

Two Voices are there: one is of the Sea,
  One of the Mountains; each a mighty voice.
  In both from age to age thou didst rejoice;
They were thy chosen music, Liberty!
There came a tyrant, and with holy glee
  Thou fought'st against him, – but hast vainly striven:
  Thou from thy Alpine holds at length art driven,
Where not a torrent murmurs heard by thee.
– Of one deep bliss thine ear hath been bereft:
Then cleave, O cleave to that which still is left;
  For, high-soul'd Maid, what sorrow would it be
That Mountain floods should thunder as before,
And Ocean bellow from his rocky shore,
  And neither awful Voice be heard by thee!

## WILLIAM WORDSWORTH
# I Travell'd Among Unknown Men

I travell'd among unknown men
  In lands beyond the sea;
Nor, England! did I know till then
  What love I bore to thee.

'Tis past, that melancholy dream!
  Nor will I quit thy shore
A second time, for still I seem
  To love thee more and more.

Among thy mountains did I feel
  The joy of my desire;
And she I cherish'd turn'd her wheel
  Beside an English fire.

Thy mornings show'd, thy nights conceal'd
  The bowers where Lucy play'd;
And thine too is the last green field
  That Lucy's eyes survey'd.


## WILLIAM WORDSWORTH

# Lines Written a Few Miles Above Tintern Abbey, on Revisiting the Banks of the Wye During a Tour, July 13, 1798

Five years have passed; five summers, with the length
Of five long winters! and again I hear
These waters, rolling from their mountain-springs
With a sweet inland murmur. – Once again
Do I behold these steep and lofty cliffs,
Which on a wild secluded scene impress
Thoughts of more deep seclusion; and connect
The landscape with the quiet of the sky.
The day is come when I again repose
Here, under this dark sycamore, and view
These plots of cottage-ground, these orchard-tufts,
Which, at this season, with their unripe fruits,
Among the woods and copses lose themselves,
Nor, with their green and simple hue, disturb
The wild green landscape. Once again I see
These hedge-rows, hardly hedge-rows, little lines
Of sportive wood run wild; these pastoral farms
Green to the very door; and wreathes of smoke
Sent up, in silence, from among the trees,
With some uncertain notice, as might seem,

Of vagrant dwellers in the houseless woods,
Or of some hermit's cave, where by his fire
The hermit sits alone.

            Though absent long,
These forms of beauty have not been to me,
As is a landscape to a blind man's eye:
But oft, in lonely rooms, and mid the din
Of towns and cities, I have owed to them,
In hours of weariness, sensations sweet,
Felt in the blood, and felt along the heart,
And passing even into my purer mind
With tranquil restoration: – feelings too
As may have had no trivial influence
On that best portion of a good man's life;
His little, nameless, unremembered acts
Of kindness and of love. Nor less, I trust,
To them I may have owed another gift,
Of aspect more sublime; that blessed mood,
In which the burthen of the mystery,
In which the heavy and the weary weight
Of all this unintelligible world
Is lighten'd: – that serene and blessed mood,
In which the affections gently lead us on,
Until, the breath of this corporeal frame,
And even the motion of our human blood
Almost suspended, we are laid asleep
In body, and become a living soul:
While with an eye made quiet by the power
Of harmony, and the deep power of joy,
We see into the life of things.

            If this
Be but a vain belief, yet, oh! how oft,
In darkness, and amid the many shapes
Of joyless day-light; when the fretful stir
Unprofitable, and the fever of the world,
Have hung upon the beatings of my heart,
How oft, in spirit, have I turned to thee
O sylvan Wye! Thou wanderer through the woods,
How often has my spirit turned to thee!

And now, with gleams of half-extinguish'd thought,
With many recognitions dim and faint,
And somewhat of a sad perplexity,
The picture of the mind revives again:
While here I stand, not only with the sense
Of present pleasure, but with pleasing thoughts
That in this moment there is life and food
For future years. And so I dare to hope
Though changed, no doubt, from what I was, when first
I came among these hills; when like a roe
I bounded o'er the mountains, by the sides
Of the deep rivers, and the lonely streams,
Wherever nature led; more like a man
Flying from something that he dreads, than one
Who sought the thing he loved. For nature then
And their glad animal movements all gone by,
To me was all in all. – I cannot paint
What then I was. The sounding cataract
Haunted me like a passion: the tall rock,
The mountain, and the deep and gloomy wood,
Their colours and their forms, were then to me
An appetite: a feeling and a love,
That had no need of a remoter charm,
By thought supplied, or any interest
Unborrowed from the eye. – That time is past,
And all its aching joys are now no more,
And all its dizzy raptures. Not for this
Faint I, nor mourn nor murmur: other gifts
Have followed, for such loss, I would believe,
Abundant recompence. For I have learned
To look on nature, not as in the hour
Of thoughtless youth, but hearing oftentimes
The still, sad music of humanity,
Not harsh nor grating, though of ample power
To chasten and subdue. And I have felt
A presence that disturbs me with the joy
Of elevated thoughts; a sense sublime
Of something far more deeply interfused,
Whose dwelling is the light of setting suns,

And the round ocean, and the living air,
And the blue sky, and in the mind of man,
A motion and a spirit, that impels
All thinking things, all objects of all thought,
And rolls through all things. Therefore am I still
A lover of the meadows and the woods,
And mountains; and of all that we behold
From this green earth; of all the mighty world
Of eye and ear, both what they half-create,
And what perceive; well pleased to recognize
In nature and the language of the sense,
The anchor of my purest thoughts, the nurse,
The guide, the guardian of my heart, and soul
Of all my moral being.

                    Nor, perchance,
If I were not thus taught, should I the more
Suffer my genial spirits to decay:
For thou art with me here upon the banks
Of this fair river; thou, my dearest Friend,
My dear, dear Friend, and in thy voice I catch
The language of my former heart, and read
My former pleasures in the shooting lights
Of thy wild eyes. Oh! yet a little while
May I behold in thee what I was once,
My dear, dear Sister! And this prayer I make,
Knowing that Nature never did betray
The heart that loved her; 'tis her privilege,
Through all the years of this our life, to lead
From joy to joy: for she can so inform
The mind that is within us, so impress
With quietness and beauty, and so feed
With lofty thoughts, that neither evil tongues,
Rash judgments, nor the sneers of selfish men,
Nor greetings where no kindness is, nor all
The dreary intercourse of daily life,
Shall e'er prevail against us, or disturb
Our chearful faith that all which we behold
Is full of blessings. Therefore let the moon
Shine on thee in thy solitary walk;

And let the misty mountain winds be free
To blow against thee: and in after years,
When these wild ecstasies shall be matured
Into a sober pleasure, when thy mind
Shall be a mansion for all lovely forms,
Thy memory be as a dwelling-place
For all sweet sounds and harmonies; Oh! then,
If solitude, or fear, or pain, or grief,
Should be thy portion, with what healing thoughts
Of tender joy wilt thou remember me,
And these my exhortations! Nor, perchance,
If I should be, where I no more can hear
Thy voice, nor catch from thy wild eyes these gleams
Of past existence, wilt thou then forget
That on the banks of this delightful stream
We stood together; and that I, so long
A worshipper of Nature, hither came,
Unwearied in that service: rather say
With warmer love, oh! with far deeper zeal
Of holier love. Nor wilt thou then forget,
That after many wanderings, many years
Of absence, these steep woods and lofty cliffs,
And this green pastoral landscape, were to me
More dear, both for themselves and for thy sake!

## PERCY BYSSHE SHELLEY

# Ozymandias of Egypt

I met a traveller from an antique land
Who said: – Two vast and trunkless legs of stone
Stand in the desert. Near them on the sand,
Half sunk, a shatter'd visage lies, whose frown
And wrinkled lip and sneer of cold command
Tell that its sculptor well those passions read

Which yet survive, stamp'd on these lifeless things,
The hand that mock'd them and the heart that fed.
And on the pedestal these words appear:
'My name is Ozymandias, king of kings:
Look on my works, ye mighty, and despair!'
Nothing beside remains: round the decay
Of that colossal wreck, boundless and bare,
The lone and level sands stretch far away.

## PERCY BYSSHE SHELLEY

# Stanzas Written in Dejection – December 1818, Near Naples

The sun is warm, the sky is clear,
The waves are dancing fast and bright,
Blue isles and snowy mountains wear
The purple noon's transparent might:
The breath of the moist earth is light
Around its unexpanded buds;
Like many a voice of one delight –
The winds', the birds', the ocean-floods' –
The city's voice itself is soft like solitude's.

I see the deep's untrampled floor
With green and purple seaweeds strown;
I see the waves upon the shore
Like light dissolved in star-showers thrown.
I sit upon the sands alone;
The lightning of the noontide ocean
Is flashing round me, and a tone
Arises from its measured motion –
How sweet, did any heart now share in my emotion!

Alas! I have nor hope nor health,
Nor peace within nor calm around;

Nor that content, surpassing wealth,
The sage in meditation found,
And walk'd with inward glory crown'd;
Nor fame, nor power, nor love, nor leisure.
Others I see whom these surround –
Smiling they live, and call life pleasure:
To me that cup has been dealt in another measure.

Yet now despair itself is mild,
Even as the winds and waters are;
I could lie down like a tired child,
And weep away the life of care
Which I have borne, and yet must bear, –
Till death like sleep might steal on me,
And I might feel in the warm air
My cheek grow cold, and hear the sea
Breathe o'er my dying brain its last monotony.

## PERCY BYSSHE SHELLEY

# Lines Written Among the Euganean Hills

Many a green isle needs must be
In the deep wide sea of Misery,
Or the mariner, worn and wan,
Never thus could voyage on
Day and night, and night and day,
Drifting on his dreary way,
With the solid darkness black
Closing round his vessel's track;
Whilst above, the sunless sky
Big with clouds, hangs heavily,
And behind the tempest fleet
Hurries on with lightning feet,
Riving sail, and cord, and plank,
Till the ship has almost drank

Death from the o'er-brimming deep,
And sinks down, down, like that sleep
When the dreamer seems to be
Weltering through eternity;
And the dim low line before
Of a dark and distant shore
Still recedes, as ever still
Longing with divided will,
But no power to seek or shun,
He is ever drifted on
O'er the unreposing wave,
To the haven of the grave.

Ay, many flowering islands lie
In the waters of wide Agony:
To such a one this morn was led
My bark, by soft winds piloted.
– 'Mid the mountains Euganean
I stood listening to the paean
With which the legion'd rooks did hail
The Sun's uprise majestical:
Gathering round with wings all hoar,
Through the dewy mist they soar
Like gray shades, till the eastern heaven
Bursts; and then – as clouds of even
Fleck'd with fire and azure, lie
In the unfathomable sky –
So their plumes of purple grain
Starr'd with drops of golden rain
Gleam above the sunlight woods,
As in silent multitudes
On the morning's fitful gale
Through the broken mist they sail;
And the vapours cloven and gleaming
Follow down the dark steep streaming,
Till all is bright, and clear, and still
Round the solitary hill.

Beneath is spread like a green sea
The waveless plain of Lombardy,

Bounded by the vaporous air,
Islanded by cities fair;
Underneath day's azure eyes,
Ocean's nursling, Venice lies, –
A peopled labyrinth of walls,
Amphitrite's destined halls,
Which her hoary sire now paves
With his blue and beaming waves.
Lo! the sun upsprings behind,
Broad, red, radiant, half-reclined
On the level quivering line
Of the waters crystalline;
And before that chasm of light,
As within a furnace bright,
Column, tower, and dome, and spire,
Shine like obelisks of fire,
Pointing with inconstant motion
From the altar of dark ocean
To the sapphire-tinted skies;
As the flames of sacrifice
From the marble shrines did rise
As to pierce the dome of gold
Where Apollo spoke of old.

Sun-girt City! thou hast been
Ocean's child, and then his queen;
Now is come a darker day,
And thou soon must be his prey,
If the power that raised thee here
Hallow so thy watery bier.
A less drear ruin then than now,
With thy conquest-branded brow
Stooping to the slave of slaves
From thy throne among the waves
Wilt thou be – when the sea-mew
Flies, as once before it flew,
O'er thine isles depopulate,
And all is in its ancient state,
Save where many a palace-gate
With green sea-flowers overgrown,

Like a rock of ocean's own,
Topples o'er the abandon'd sea
As the tides change sullenly.
The fisher on his watery way,
Wandering at the close of day,
Will spread his sail and seize his oar
Till he pass the gloomy shore,
Lest thy dead should, from their sleep,
Bursting o'er the starlight deep,
Lead a rapid masque of death
O'er the waters of his path.

Noon descends around me now:
'Tis the noon of autumn's glow,
When a soft and purple mist
Like a vaporous amethyst,
Or an air-dissolvèd star
Mingling light and fragrance, far
From the curved horizon's bound
To the point of heaven's profound,
Fills the overflowing sky,
And the plains that silent lie
Underneath; the leaves unsodden
Where the infant Frost has trodden
With his morning-wingèd feet
Whose bright print is gleaming yet;
And the red and golden vines
Piercing with their trellised lines
The rough, dark-skirted wilderness;
The dun and bladed grass no less,
Pointing from this hoary tower
In the windless air; the flower
Glimmering at my feet; the line
Of the olive-sandall'd Apennine
In the south dimly islanded;
And the Alps, whose snows are spread
High between the clouds and sun;
And of living things each one;
And my spirit, which so long
Darken'd this swift stream of song, –

Interpenetrated lie
By the glory of the sky;
Be it love, light, harmony,
Odour, or the soul of all
Which from heaven like dew doth fall,
Or the mind which feeds this verse,
Peopling the lone universe.

   Noon descends, and after noon
Autumn's evening meets me soon,
Leading the infantine moon
And that one star, which to her
Almost seems to minister
Half the crimson light she brings
From the sunset's radiant springs:
And the soft dreams of the morn
(Which like wingèd winds had borne
To that silent isle, which lies
'Mid remember'd agonies,
The frail bark of this lone being),
Pass, to other sufferers fleeing,
And its ancient pilot, Pain,
Sits beside the helm again.

   Other flowering isles must be
In the sea of Life and Agony:
Other spirits float and flee
O'er that gulf: ev'n now, perhaps,
On some rock the wild wave wraps,
With folding wings they waiting sit
For my bark, to pilot it
To some calm and blooming cove,
Where for me, and those I love,
May a windless bower be built,
Far from passion, pain, and guilt,
In a dell 'mid lawny hills
Which the wild sea-murmur fills,
And soft sunshine, and the sound
Of old forests echoing round,
And the light and smell divine

Of all flowers that breathe and shine.
– We may live so happy there,
That the Spirits of the Air
Envying us, may ev'n entice
To our healing paradise
The polluting multitude:
But their rage would be subdued
By that clime divine and calm,
And the winds whose wings rain balm
On the uplifted soul, and leaves
Under which the bright sea heaves;
While each breathless interval
In their whisperings musical
The inspirèd soul supplies
With its own deep melodies;
And the Love which heals all strife
Circling, like the breath of life,
All things in that sweet abode
With its own mild brotherhood: –
They, not it, would change; and soon
Every sprite beneath the moon
Would repent its envy vain,
And the Earth grow young again!


## GEORGE GORDON BYRON

# The Isles of Greece

The isles of Greece! the isles of Greece
  Where burning Sappho loved and sung,
Where grew the arts of war and peace,
  Where Delos rose, and Phoebus sprung!
Eternal summer gilds them yet,
But all, except their sun, is set.

The Scian and the Teian muse,
  The hero's harp, the lover's lute,
Have found the fame your shores refuse:
  Their place of birth alone is mute
To sounds which echo further west
Than your sires' 'Islands of the Blest'.

The mountains look on Marathon –
  And Marathon looks on the sea;
And musing there an hour alone,
  I dream'd that Greece might still be free;
For standing on the Persians' grave,
I could not deem myself a slave.

A king sate on the rocky brow
  Which looks o'er sea-born Salamis;
And ships, by thousands, lay below,
  And men in nations; – all were his!
He counted them at break of day –
And when the sun set, where were they?

And where are they? and where art thou,
  My country? On thy voiceless shore
The heroic lay is tuneless now –
  The heroic bosom beats no more!
And must thy lyre, so long divine,
Degenerate into hands like mine?

'Tis something in the dearth of fame,
  Though link'd among a fetter'd race,
To feel at least a patriot's shame,
  Even as I sing, suffuse my face;
For what is left the poet here?
For Greeks a blush – for Greece a tear.

Must we but weep o'er days more blest?
  Must we but blush? – Our fathers bled.
Earth! render back from out thy breast
  A remnant of our Spartan dead!
Of the three hundred grant but three,
To make a new Thermopylae!

What, silent still? and silent all?
  Ah! no; – the voices of the dead
Sound like a distant torrent's fall,
  And answer, 'Let one living head,
But one, arise, – we come, we come!'
'Tis but the living who are dumb.

In vain – in vain: strike other chords;
  Fill high the cup with Samian wine!
Leave battles to the Turkish hordes,
  And shed the blood of Scio's vine:
Hark! rising to the ignoble call –
How answers each bold Bacchanal!

You have the Pyrrhic dance as yet;
  Where is the Pyrrhic phalanx gone?
Of two such lessons, why forget
  The nobler and the manlier one?
You have the letters Cadmus gave –
Think ye he meant them for a slave?

Fill high the bowl with Samian wine!
  We will not think of themes like these!
It made Anacreon's song divine:
  He served – but served Polycrates –
A tyrant; but our masters then
Were still, at least, our countrymen.

The tyrant of the Chersonese
  Was freedom's best and bravest friend;
That tyrant was Miltiades!
  O that the present hour would lend
Another despot of the kind!
Such chains as his were sure to bind.

Fill high the bowl with Samian wine!
  On Suli's rock, and Parga's shore,
Exists the remnant of a line
  Such as the Doric mothers bore;
And there, perhaps, some seed is sown,
The Heracleidan blood might own.

Trust not for freedom to the Franks –
  They have a king who buys and sells;
In native swords and native ranks
  The only hope of courage dwells:
But Turkish force and Latin fraud
Would break your shield, however broad.

Fill high the bowl with Samian wine!
  Our virgins dance beneath the shade –
I see their glorious black eyes shine;
  But gazing on each glowing maid,
My own the burning tear-drop laves,
To think such breasts must suckle slaves.

Place me on Sunium's marbled steep,
  Where nothing, save the waves and I,
May hear our mutual murmurs sweep;
  There, swan-like, let me sing and die:
A land of slaves shall ne'er be mine –
Dash down yon cup of Samian wine!

## FITZ-GREENE HALLECK

# Connecticut

– Still her gray rocks tower above the sea
  That crouches at their feet, a conquered wave;
'T is a rough land of earth, and stone, and tree,
  Where breathes no castled lord or cabined slave;
Where thoughts, and tongues, and hands are bold and free,
  And friends will find a welcome, foes a grave;
And where none kneel, save when to Heaven they pray,
Nor even then, unless in their own way.

Theirs is a pure republic, wild, yet strong,
  A 'fierce democracie', where all are true
To what themselves have voted – right or wrong –
  And to their laws, denominated blue;
(If red, they might to Draco's code belong);
  A vestal state, which power could not subdue,
Nor promise win – like her own eagle's nest,
Sacred – the San Marino of the West.

A justice of the peace, for the time being,
  They bow to, but may turn him out next year:
They reverence their priest, but disagreeing
  In price or creed, dismiss him without fear;
They have a natural talent for foreseeing
  And knowing all things; and should Park appear
From his long tour in Africa, to show
The Niger's source, they'd meet him with – 'we know!'

They love their land, because it is their own,
  And scorn to give aught other reason why;
Would shake hands with a king upon his throne
  And think it kindness to his majesty;
A stubborn race, fearing and flattering none.
  Such are they nurtured, such they live and die:
All – but a few apostates, who are meddling
With merchandise, pounds, shillings, pence and peddling;

Or wandering through the southern countries teaching
  The A B C from Webster's spelling-book;
Gallant and godly, making love and preaching,
  And gaining, by what they call 'hook and crook',
And what the moralists call over-reaching,
  A decent living. The Virginians look
Upon them with as favorable eyes
As Gabriel on the devil in Paradise.

But these are but their outcasts. View them near
  At home, where all their worth and pride is placed;
And there their hospitable fires burn clear,
  And there the lowliest farmhouse hearth is graced

With manly hearts, in piety sincere,
  Faithful in love, in honor stern and chaste,
In friendship warm and true, in danger brave,
Beloved in life, and sainted in the grave.

And minds have there been nurtured, whose control
  Is felt even in the nation's destiny;
Men who swayed senates with a statesman's soul,
  And looked on armies with a leader's eye;
Names that adorn and dignify the scroll,
  Whose leaves contain their country's history,
And tales of love and war – listen to one
Of the Green-Mountaineer – the Stark of Bennington.

When on that field his band the Hessians fought,
  Briefly he spoke before the fight began:
'Soldiers! Those German gentlemen are bought
  For four pounds eight and sevenpence per man,
By England's king; a bargain, as is thought.
  Are we worth more? Let's prove it now we can;
For we must beat them, boys, ere set of sun,
Or Mary Stark 's a widow.' It was done.

Hers are not Tempe's nor Arcadia's spring,
  Nor the long summer of Cathayan vales,
The vines, the flowers, the air, the skies, that fling
  Such wild enchantment o'er Boccaccio's tales
Of Florence and the Arno; yet the wing
  Of life's best angel, Health, is on her gales
Through sun and snow; and, in the autumn time
Earth has no purer and no lovelier clime.

Her clear, warm heaven at noon, – the mist that shrouds
  Her twilight hills – her cool and starry eves,
The glorious splendor of her sunset clouds,
  The rainbow beauty of her forest leaves,
Come o'er the eye, in solitude and crowds,
  Where'er his web of song her poet weaves;
And his mind's brightest vision but displays
The autumn scenery of his boyhood's days.

And when you dream of woman, and her love;
  Her truth, her tenderness, her gentle power;
The maiden, listening in the moonlight grove,
  The mother, smiling in her infant's bower;
Forms, features, worshipped while we breathe or move,
  Be by some spirit of your dreaming hour
Borne, like Loretto's chapel, through the air
To the green land I sing, then wake, you'll find them there.

## FITZ-GREENE HALLECK

# Alnwick Castle

Home of the Percys' high-born race,
  Home of their beautiful and brave,
Alike their birth and burial place,
  Their cradle and their grave!
Still sternly o'er the castle gate
Their house's Lion stands in state,
  As in his proud departed hours;
And warriors frown in stone on high,
And feudal banners 'flout the sky'
  Above his princely towers.

A gentle hill its side inclines,
  Lovely in England's fadeless green,
To meet the quiet stream which winds
  Through this romantic scene
As silently and sweetly still,
As when, at evening, on that hill,
  While summer's wind blew soft and low,
Seated by gallant Hotspur's side,
His Katherine was a happy bride,
  A thousand years ago.

Gaze on the Abbey's ruined pile:
  Does not the succoring ivy, keeping
Her watch around it, seem to smile,
  As o'er a loved one sleeping?
One solitary turret gray
  Still tells, in melancholy glory,
The legend of the Cheviot day,
  The Percys' proudest border story.
That day its roof was triumph's arch;
  Then rang, from isle to pictured dome,
The light step of the soldier's march,
  The music of the trump and drum;
And babe, and sire, the old, the young,
And the monk's hymn, and minstrel's song,
And woman's pure kiss, sweet and long,
  Welcomed her warrior home.

Wild roses by the Abbey towers
  Are gay in their young bud and bloom:
They were born of a race of funeral flowers
That garlanded, in long-gone hours,
  A templar's knightly tomb.
He died, the sword in his mailed hand,
On the holiest spot of the Blessed land,
  Where the Cross was damped with his dying breath,
When blood ran free as festal wine,
And the sainted air of Palestine
  Was thick with the darts of death.

Wise with the lore of centuries,
What tales, if there be 'tongues in trees',
  Those giant oaks could tell,
Of beings born and buried here;
Tales of the peasant and the peer,
Tales of the bridal and the bier,
  The welcome and farewell,
Since on their boughs the startled bird
First, in her twilight slumbers, heard
  The Norman's curfew-bell!

I wandered through the lofty halls
　Trod by the Percys of old fame,
And traced upon the chapel walls
　Each high heroic name,
From him who once his standard set
Where now, o'er mosque and minaret,
　Glitter the Sultan's crescent moons;
To him who, when a younger son,
Fought for King George at Lexington,
　A major of dragoons.

That last half stanza – it has dashed
　From my warm lips the sparkling cup;
The light that o'er my eyebeam flashed,
　The power that bore my spirit up
Above this bank-note world – is gone;
And Alnwick's but a market town,
And this, alas! its market day,
And beasts and borderers throng the way;
Oxen and bleating lambs in lots,
Northumbrian boors and plaided Scots,
　Men in the coal and cattle line;
From Teviot's bard and hero land,
From royal Berwick's beach of sand,
From Wooller, Morpeth, Hexham, and
　Newcastle-upon-Tyne.

These are not the romantic times
So beautiful in Spenser's rhymes,
　So dazzling to the dreaming boy:
Ours are the days of fact, not fable,
Of knights, but not of the round table,
　Of Bailie Jarvie, not Rob Roy:
'T is what 'our President' Monroe
　Has called 'the era of good feeling':
The Highlander, the bitterest foe
To modern laws, has felt their blow,
Consented to be taxed, and vote,
And put on pantaloons and coat,
　And leave off cattle-stealing:

Lord Stafford mines for coal and salt,
The Duke of Norfolk deals in malt,
  The Douglas in red herrings;
And noble name and cultured land,
Palace, and park, and vassal band,
Are powerless to the notes of hand
  Of Rothschild or the Barings.

The age of bargaining, said Burke,
Has come: to-day the turbaned Turk
(Sleep, Richard of the lion heart!
Sleep on, nor from your cerements start),
  Is England's friend and fast ally;
The Moslem tramples on the Greek,
  And on the Cross and altar-stone,
  And Christendom looks tamely on,
And hears the Christian maiden shriek,
  And sees the Christian father die;
And not a sabre-blow is given
For Greece and fame, for faith and heaven,
  By Europe's craven chivalry.

You'll ask if yet the Percy lives
  In the armed pomp of feudal state?
The present representatives
  Of Hotspur and his 'gentle Kate',
Are some half-dozen serving-men
In the drab coat of William Penn;
  A chambermaid, whose lip and eye,
And cheek, and brown hair, bright and curling,
  Spoke nature's aristocracy;
And one, half groom, half seneschal,
Who bowed me through court, bower, and hall,
From donjon-keep to turret wall,
  For ten-and-sixpence sterling.

## JAMES CLARENCE MANGAN

# Siberia

In Siberia's wastes
The ice-wind's breath
Woundeth like the toothed steel;
Lost Siberia doth reveal
Only blight and death.

Blight and death alone.
No Summer shines.
Night is interblent with Day.
In Siberia's wastes alway
The blood blackens, the heart pines.

In Siberia's wastes
No tears are shed,
For they freeze within the brain.
Nought is felt but dullest pain,
Pain acute, yet dead;

Pain as in a dream,
When years go by
Funeral-paced, yet fugitive,
When man lives, and doth not live,
Doth not live – nor die.

In Siberia's wastes
Are sands and rocks,
Nothing blooms of green or soft,
But the snow-peaks rise aloft
And the gaunt ice-blocks.

And the exile there
Is one with those;
They are part, and he is part,
For the sands are in his heart,
And the killing snows.

Therefore, in those wastes
None curse the Czar.
Each man's tongue is cloven by
The North Blast, that heweth nigh
with sharp scymitar.

## WILLIAM MORRIS

# Iceland First Seen

Lo from our loitering ship a new land at last to be seen;
Toothed rocks down the side of the firth on the east guard
a weary wide lea,
And black slope the hillsides above, striped adown with
their desolate green:
And a peak rises up on the west from the meeting of
cloud and of sea,
Foursquare from base unto point like the building of Gods
that have been,
The last of that waste of the mountains all cloud-wreathed
and snow-flecked and grey,
And bright with the dawn that began just now at the
ending of day.

Ah! what came we forth for to see that our hearts are so
hot with desire?
Is it enough for our rest, the sight of this desolate strand,
And the mountain-waste voiceless as death but for winds
that may sleep not nor tire?
Why do we long to wend forth through the length and
breadth of a land,
Dreadful with grinding of ice, and record of scarce hidden
fire,
But that there 'mid the grey grassy dales sore scarred by
the ruining streams

Lives the tale of the Northland of old and the undying glory
of dreams?

O land, as some cave by the sea where the treasures of old
have been laid,
The sword it may be of a king whose name was the
turning of fight;
Or the staff of some wise of the world that many things
made and unmade,
Or the ring of a woman maybe whose woe is grown wealth
and delight.
No wheat and no wine grows above it, no orchard for
blossom and shade;
The few ships that sail by its blackness but deem it the
mouth of a grave;
Yet sure when the world shall awaken, this too shall be
mighty to save.

Or rather, O land, if a marvel it seemeth that men ever
sought
Thy wastes for a field and a garden fulfilled of all wonder
and doubt,
And feasted amidst of the winter when the fight of the year
had been fought,
Whose plunder all gathered together was little to babble
about;
Cry aloud from thy wastes, O thou land, 'Not for this nor
for that was I wrought.
Amid waning of realms and of riches and death of things
worshipped and sure,
I abide here the spouse of a God, and I made and I make
and endure.'

O Queen of the grief without knowledge, of the courage
that may not avail,
Of the longing that may not attain, of the love that shall
never forget,
More joy than the gladness of laughter thy voice hath
amidst of its wail:

More hope than of pleasure fulfilled amidst of thy blindness is set;
More glorious than gaining of all thine unfaltering hand that shall fail:
For what is the mark on thy brow but the brand that thy Brynhild doth bear?
Love once, and loved and undone by a love that no ages outwear.

Ah! when thy Balder comes back, and bears from the heart of the Sun
Peace and the healing of pain, and the wisdom that waiteth no more;
And the lilies are laid on thy brow 'mid the crown of the deeds thou hast done;
And the roses spring up by thy feet that the rocks of the wilderness wore:
Ah! when thy Balder comes back and we gather the gains he hath won,
Shall we not linger a little to talk of thy sweetness of old,
Yea, turn back awhile to thy travail whence the Gods stood aloof to behold?

## JAMES THOMSON

# In the Train

As we rush, as we rush in the Train,
The trees and the houses go wheeling back,
But the starry heavens above the plain
Come flying on our track.

All the beautiful stars of the sky,
The silver doves of the forest of Night,

Over the dull earth swarm and fly,
Companions of our flight.

We will rush ever on without fear;
Let the goal be far, the flight be fleet!
For we carry the Heavens with us, dear,
While the Earth slips from our feet!

## EUGENE FIELD

# In Amsterdam

Mynheer Hans Von Der Bloom has got
A majazin in Kalverstraat,
Where one may buy for sordid gold
Wares quaint and curious, new and old.
Here are antiquities galore, –
The jewels which Dutch monarchs wore,
Swords, teacups, helmets, platters, clocks,
Bright Dresden jars, dull Holland crocks,
And all those joys I might rehearse
That please the eye, but wreck the purse.

I most admired an ancient bed,
With ornate carvings at its head, –
A massive frame of dingy oak,
Whose curious size and mould bespoke
Prodigious age. 'How much?' I cried.
'Ein tousand gildens,' Hans replied;
And then the honest Dutchman said
A king once owned that glorious bed, –
King Fritz der Foorst, of blessed fame,
Had owned and slept within the same!

Then long I stood and mutely gazed,
By reminiscent splendors dazed,
And I had bought it right away,
Had I the wherewithal to pay.
But, lacking of the needed pelf,
I thus discoursed within myself:
'O happy Holland! where's the bliss
That can approximate to this
Possession of the rare antique
Which maniacs hanker for and seek?
My native land is full of stuff
That's good, but is not old enough.
Alas! it has no oaken beds
Wherein have slumbered royal heads,
No relic on whose face we see
The proof of grand antiquity.'

Thus reasoned I a goodly spell
Until, perchance, my vision fell
Upon a trademark at the head
Of Fritz der Foorst's old oaken bed, –
A rampant wolverine, and round
This strange device these words I found:
'Patent Antique. Birkey & Gay,
Grand Rapids, Michigan, U. S. A.'

At present I'm not saying much
About the simple, guileless Dutch;
And as it were a loathsome spot
I keep away from Kalverstraat,
Determined when I want a bed
In which hath slept a royal head
I'll patronize no middleman,
But deal direct with Michigan.

### HENRY CHARLES BEECHING

# Going Downhill on a Bicycle:
# A Boy's Song

With lifted feet, hands still
I am poised, and down the hill
Dart, with heedful mind;
The air goes by in a wind.

Swifter and yet more swift,
Till the heart with a mighty lift
Makes the lungs laugh, the throat cry: –
'O bird, see; see, bird, I fly.

'Is this, is this your joy?
O bird, then I, though a boy
For a golden moment share
Your feathery life in air!'

Say, heart, is there aught like this
In a world that is full of bliss?
'Tis more than skating, bound
Steel-shod to the level ground.

Speed slackens now, I float
Awhile in my airy boat;
Till, when the wheels scarce crawl,
My feet to the treadles fall.

Alas, that the longest hill
Must end in a vale; but still,
Who climbs with toil, wheresoe'er,
Shall find wings waiting there.

# WALT WHITMAN

# Passage to India

[1]

Singing my days,
Singing the great achievements of the present,
Singing the strong, light works of engineers,
Our modern wonders, (the antique ponderous Seven outvied,)
In the Old World, the east, the Suez canal,
The New by its mighty railroad spann'd,
The seas inlaid with eloquent, gentle wires,
I sound, to commence, the cry, with thee, O soul,
The Past! the Past! the Past!

The Past! the dark, unfathom'd retrospect!
The teeming gulf! the sleepers and the shadows!
The past! the infinite greatness of the past!
For what is the present, after all, but a growth out of the
    past?
(As a projectile, form'd, impell'd, passing a certain line, still
    keeps on,
So the present, utterly form'd, impell'd by the past.)

[2]

Passage, O soul, to India!
Eclaircise the myths Asiatic – the primitive fables.

Not you alone, proud truths of the world!
Nor you alone, ye facts of modern science!
But myths and fables of eld – Asia's, Africa's fables!
The far-darting beams of the spirit! – the unloos'd dreams!
The deep diving bibles and legends;
The daring plots of the poets – the elder religions;
– O you temples fairer than lilies, pour'd over by the rising
    sun!
O you fables, spurning the known, eluding the hold of the
    known, mounting to heaven!

You lofty and dazzling towers, pinnacled, red as roses,
   burnish'd with gold!
Towers of fables immortal, fashion'd from mortal dreams!
You too I welcome, and fully, the same as the rest;
You too with joy I sing.


[3]

Passage to India!
Lo, soul! seest thou not God's purpose from the first?
The earth to be spann'd, connected by net-work,
The people to become brothers and sisters,
The races, neighbors, to marry and be given in marriage,
The oceans to be cross'd, the distant brought near,
The lands to be welded together.

(A worship new, I sing,
You captains, voyagers, explorers, yours!
You engineers! you architects, machinists, yours!
You, not for trade or transportation only,
But in God's name, and for thy sake, O soul.)


[4]

Passage to India!
Lo, soul, for thee, of tableaus twain,
I see, in one, the Suez canal initiated, open'd,
I see the procession of steamships, the Empress Eugenie's
   leading the van;
I mark, from on deck, the strange landscape, the pure sky,
   the level sand in the distance;
I pass swiftly the picturesque groups, the workmen gather'd,
The gigantic dredging machines.

In one, again, different, (yet thine, all thine, O soul, the
   same,)
I see over my own continent the Pacific Railroad,
   surmounting every barrier;
I see continual trains of cars winding along the Platte,
   carrying freight and passengers;
I hear the locomotives rushing and roaring, and the shrill
   steam-whistle,

I hear the echoes reverberate through the grandest scenery in
the world;
I cross the Laramie plains – I note the rocks in grotesque
shapes – the buttes;
I see the plentiful larkspur and wild onions – the barren,
colorless, sage-deserts;
I see in glimpses afar, or towering immediately above me, the
great mountains – I see the Wind River and the Wahsatch
mountains;
I see the Monument mountain and the Eagle's Nest – I pass
the Promontory – I ascend the Nevadas;
I scan the noble Elk mountain, and wind around its base;
I see the Humboldt range – I thread the valley and cross the
river,
I see the clear waters of Lake Tahoe – I see forests of majestic
pines,
Or, crossing the great desert, the alkaline plains, I behold
enchanting mirages of waters and meadows;
Marking through these, and after all, in duplicate slender
lines,
Bridging the three or four thousand miles of land travel,
Tying the Eastern to the Western sea,
The road between Europe and Asia.

(Ah Genoese, thy dream! thy dream!
Centuries after thou art laid in thy grave,
The shore thou foundest verifies thy dream!)

[5]

Passage to India!
Struggles of many a captain – tales of many a sailor dead!
Over my mood, stealing and spreading they come,
Like clouds and cloudlets in the unreach'd sky.

Along all history, down the slopes,
As a rivulet running, sinking now, and now again to the
surface rising,
A ceaseless thought, a varied train – Lo, soul! to thee, thy
sight, they rise,

The plans, the voyages again, the expeditions:
Again Vasco de Gama sails forth;
Again the knowledge gain'd, the mariner's compass,
Lands found, and nations born – thou born, America, (a
    hemisphere unborn,)
For purpose vast, man's long probation fill'd,
Thou, rondure of the world, at last accomplish'd.

[6]
O, vast Rondure, swimming in space!
Cover'd all over with visible power and beauty!
Alternate light and day, and the teeming, spiritual darkness;
Unspeakable, high processions of sun and moon, and countless
    stars, above;
Below, the manifold grass and waters, animals, mountains,
    trees;
With inscrutable purpose – some hidden, prophetic intention;
Now, first, it seems, my thought begins to span thee.

Down from the gardens of Asia, descending, radiating,
Adam and Eve appear, then their myriad progeny after them,
Wandering, yearning, curious – with restless explorations,
With questionings, baffled, formless, feverish – with never-
    happy hearts,
With that sad, incessant refrain, Wherefore, unsatisfied Soul?
    and
Whither, O mocking Life?

Ah, who shall soothe these feverish children?
Who justify these restless explorations?
Who speak the secret of impassive Earth?
Who bind it to us? What is this separate Nature, so
    unnatural?
What is this Earth, to our affections? (unloving earth, without
    a throb to answer ours;
Cold earth, the place of graves.)

Yet, soul, be sure the first intent remains – and shall be
    carried out;
(Perhaps even now the time has arrived.)

After the seas are all cross'd, (as they seem already cross'd,)
After the great captains and engineers have accomplish'd their
    work,
After the noble inventors – after the scientists, the chemist,
    the geologist, ethnologist,
Finally shall come the Poet, worthy that name;
The true Son of God shall come, singing his songs.

Then, not your deeds only, O voyagers, O scientists and
    inventors, shall be justified,
All these hearts, as of fretted children, shall be sooth'd,
All affection shall be fully responded to – the secret shall be
    told;
All these separations and gaps shall be taken up, and hook'd
    and link'd together;
The whole Earth – this cold, impassive, voiceless Earth, shall
    be completely justified;
Trinitas divine shall be gloriously accomplish'd and compacted
    by the Son of God, the poet,
(He shall indeed pass the straits and conquer the mountains,
He shall double the Cape of Good Hope to some purpose;)
Nature and Man shall be disjoin'd and diffused no more,
The true Son of God shall absolutely fuse them.

[7]
Year at whose open'd, wide-flung door I sing!
Year of the purpose accomplish'd!
Year of the marriage of continents, climates and oceans!
(No mere Doge of Venice now, wedding the Adriatic;)
I see, O year, in you, the vast terraqueous globe, given, and
    giving all,
Europe to Asia, Africa join'd, and they to the New World;
The lands, geographies, dancing before you, holding a festival
    garland,
As brides and bridegrooms hand in hand.

[8]
Passage to India!
Cooling airs from Caucasus far, soothing cradle of man,
The river Euphrates flowing, the past lit up again.

Lo, soul, the retrospect, brought forward;
The old, most populous, wealthiest of Earth's lands,
The streams of the Indus and the Ganges, and their many
    affluents;
(I, my shores of America walking to-day, behold, resuming
    all,)
The tale of Alexander, on his warlike marches, suddenly
    dying,
On one side China, and on the other side Persia and Arabia,
To the south the great seas, and the Bay of Bengal;
The flowing literatures, tremendous epics, religions, castes,
Old occult Brahma, interminably far back – the tender and
    junior Buddha,
Central and southern empires, and all their belongings,
    possessors,
The wars of Tamerlane, the reign of Aurungzebe,
The traders, rulers, explorers, Moslems, Venetians, Byzantium,
    the Arabs, Portuguese,
The first travelers, famous yet, Marco Polo, Batouta the Moor,
Doubts to be solv'd, the map incognita, blanks to be fill'd,
The foot of man unstay'd, the hands never at rest,
Thyself, O soul, that will not brook a challenge.

[9]
The medieval navigators rise before me,
The world of 1492, with its awaken'd enterprise;
Something swelling in humanity now like the sap of the earth
    in spring,
The sunset splendor of chivalry declining.

And who art thou, sad shade?
Gigantic, visionary, thyself a visionary,
With majestic limbs, and pious, beaming eyes,
Spreading around, with every look of thine, a golden world,
Enhuing it with gorgeous hues.

As the chief histrion,
Down to the footlights walks, in some great scena,
Dominating the rest, I see the Admiral himself,
(History's type of courage, action, faith;)

Behold him sail from Palos, leading his little fleet;
His voyage behold – his return – his great fame,
His misfortunes, calumniators – behold him a prisoner,
    chain'd,
Behold his dejection, poverty, death.

(Curious, in time, I stand, noting the efforts of heroes;
Is the deferment long? bitter the slander, poverty, death?
Lies the seed unreck'd for centuries in the ground? Lo! to
    God's due occasion,
Uprising in the night, it sprouts, blooms,
And fills the earth with use and beauty.)

[10]

Passage indeed, O soul, to primal thought!
Not lands and seas alone – thy own clear freshness,
The young maturity of brood and bloom;
To realms of budding bibles.

O soul, repressless, I with thee, and thou with me,
Thy circumnavigation of the world begin;
Of man, the voyage of his mind's return,
To reason's early paradise,
Back, back to wisdom's birth, to innocent intuitions,
Again with fair Creation.

[11]

O we can wait no longer!
We too take ship, O soul!
Joyous, we too launch out on trackless seas!
Fearless, for unknown shores, on waves of extasy to sail,
Amid the wafting winds, (thou pressing me to thee, I thee to
    me, O soul,)
Caroling free – singing our song of God,
Chanting our chant of pleasant exploration.

With laugh, and many a kiss,
(Let others deprecate – let others weep for sin, remorse,
    humiliation;)
O soul, thou pleasest me – I thee.

Ah, more than any priest, O soul, we too believe in God;
But with the mystery of God we dare not dally.

O soul, thou pleasest me – I thee;
Sailing these seas, or on the hills, or waking in the night,
Thoughts, silent thoughts, of Time, and Space, and Death, like
    waters flowing,
Bear me, indeed, as through the regions infinite,
Whose air I breathe, whose ripples hear – lave me all over;
Bathe me, O God, in thee – mounting to thee,
I and my soul to range in range of thee.

O Thou transcendant!
Nameless – the fibre and the breath!
Light of the light – shedding forth universes – thou centre of
    them!
Thou mightier centre of the true, the good, the loving!
Thou moral, spiritual fountain! affection's source! thou
    reservoir!
(O pensive soul of me! O thirst unsatisfied! waitest not there?
Waitest not haply for us, somewhere there, the Comrade
    perfect?)
Thou pulse! thou motive of the stars, suns, systems,
That, circling, move in order, safe, harmonious,
Athwart the shapeless vastnesses of space!

How should I think – how breathe a single breath – how
    speak – if, out of myself,
I could not launch, to those, superior universes?

Swiftly I shrivel at the thought of God,
At Nature and its wonders, Time and Space and Death,
But that I, turning, call to thee, O soul, thou actual Me,
And lo! thou gently masterest the orbs,
Thou matest Time, smilest content at Death,
And fillest, swellest full, the vastnesses of Space.

Greater than stars or suns,
Bounding, O soul, thou journeyest forth;
– What love, than thine and ours could wider amplify?

What aspirations, wishes, outvie thine and ours, O soul?
What dreams of the ideal? what plans of purity, perfection,
  strength?
What cheerful willingness, for others' sake, to give up all?
For others' sake to suffer all?

Reckoning ahead, O soul, when thou, the time achiev'd,
(The seas all cross'd, weather'd the capes, the voyage done,)
Surrounded, copest, frontest God, yieldest, the aim attain'd,
As, fill'd with friendship, love complete, the Elder Brother
  found,
The Younger melts in fondness in his arms.


[12]
Passage to more than India!
Are thy wings plumed indeed for such far flights?
O Soul, voyagest thou indeed on voyages like these?
Disportest thou on waters such as these?
Soundest below the Sanscrit and the Vedas?
Then have thy bent unleash'd.

Passage to you, your shores, ye aged fierce enigmas!
Passage to you, to mastership of you, ye strangling problems!
You, strew'd with the wrecks of skeletons, that, living, never
  reach'd you.


[13]
Passage to more than India!
O secret of the earth and sky!
Of you, O waters of the sea! O winding creeks and rivers!
Of you, O woods and fields! Of you, strong mountains of my
  land!
Of you, O prairies! Of you, gray rocks!
O morning red! O clouds! O rain and snows!
O day and night, passage to you!

O sun and moon, and all you stars! Sirius and Jupiter!
Passage to you!

Passage – immediate passage! the blood burns in my veins!

Away, O soul! hoist instantly the anchor!
Cut the hawsers – haul out – shake out every sail!
Have we not stood here like trees in the ground long enough?
Have we not grovell'd here long enough, eating and drinking
   like mere brutes?
Have we not darken'd and dazed ourselves with books long
   enough?

Sail forth! steer for the deep waters only!
Reckless, O soul, exploring, I with thee, and thou with me;
For we are bound where mariner has not yet dared to go,
And we will risk the ship, ourselves and all.

O my brave soul!
O farther, farther sail!
O daring joy, but safe! Are they not all the seas of God?
O farther, farther, farther sail!


## WALT WHITMAN

# To a Locomotive in Winter


Thee for my recitative!
Thee in the driving storm, even as now – the snow – the
   winter-day declining;
Thee in thy panoply, thy measured dual throbbing, and thy
   beat convulsive;
Thy black cylindric body, golden brass, and silvery steel;
Thy ponderous side-bars, parallel and connecting rods,
   gyrating, shuttling at thy sides;
Thy metrical, now swelling pant and roar – now tapering in
   the distance;
Thy great protruding head-light, fix'd in front;
Thy long, pale, floating vapor-pennants, tinged with delicate
   purple;
The dense and murky clouds out-belching from thy smoke-
   stack;

Thy knitted frame – thy springs and valves – the tremulous
 twinkle of thy wheels;
Thy train of cars behind, obedient, merrily-following,
Through gale or calm, now swift, now slack, yet steadily
 careering:
Type of the modern! emblem of motion and power! pulse of
 the continent!
For once, come serve the Muse, and merge in verse, even as
 here I see thee,
With storm, and buffeting gusts of wind, and falling snow;
By day, thy warning, ringing bell to sound its notes,
By night, thy silent signal lamps to swing.

Fierce-throated beauty!
Roll through my chant, with all thy lawless music! thy
 swinging lamps at night;
Thy piercing, madly-whistled laughter! thy echoes, rumbling
 like an earthquake, rousing all!
Law of thyself complete, thine own track firmly holding;
(No sweetness debonair of tearful harp or glib piano thine,)
Thy trills of shrieks by rocks and hills return'd,
Launch'd o'er the prairies wide – across the lakes,
To the free skies, unpent, and glad, and strong.

## OSCAR WILDE

# Impression du Voyage

The sea was sapphire coloured, and the sky
 Burned like a heated opal through the air,
 We hoisted sail; the wind was blowing fair
For the blue lands that to the eastward lie.
From the steep prow I marked with quickening eye
 Zakynthos, every olive grove and creek,
 Ithaca's cliff, Lycaon's snowy peak,

And all the flower-strewn hills of Arcady.
The flapping of the sail against the mast,
  The ripple of the water on the side,
  The ripple of girls' laughter at the stern,
The only sounds: – when 'gan the West to burn,
  And a red sun upon the seas to ride,
  I stood upon the soil of Greece at last!


## OSCAR WILDE

# Rome Unvisited

[1]
The corn has turned from grey to red,
  Since first my spirit wandered forth
  From the drear cities of the north,
And to Italia's mountains fled.

And here I set my face towards home,
  For all my pilgrimage is done,
  Although, methinks, yon blood-red sun
Marshals the way to Holy Rome.

O Blessed Lady, who dost hold
  Upon the seven hills thy reign!
  O Mother without blot or stain,
Crowned with bright crowns of triple gold!

O Roma, Roma, at thy feet
  I lay this barren gift of song!
  For, ah! the way is steep and long
That leads unto thy sacred street.

[2]
And yet what joy it were for me
  To turn my feet unto the south,

And journeying towards the Tiber mouth
To kneel again at Fiesole!

And wandering through the tangled pines
  That break the gold of Arno's stream,
  To see the purple mist and gleam
Of morning on the Apennines.

By many a vineyard-hidden home,
  Orchard, and olive-garden grey,
  Till from the drear Campagna's way
The seven hills bear up the dome!

[3]

A pilgrim from the northern seas –
  What joy for me to seek alone
  The wondrous Temple, and the throne
Of Him who holds the awful keys!

When, bright with purple and with gold,
  Come priest and holy Cardinal,
  And borne above the heads of all
The gentle Shepherd of the Fold.

O joy to see before I die
  The only God-anointed King,
  And hear the silver trumpets ring
A triumph as He passes by!

Or at the altar of the shrine
  Holds high the mystic sacrifice,
  And shows a God to human eyes
Beneath the veil of bread and wine.

[4]

For lo, what changes time can bring!
  The cycles of revolving years
  May free my heart from all its fears, –
And teach my lips a song to sing.

Before yon field of trembling gold
  Is garnered into dusty sheaves,
  Or ere the autumn's scarlet leaves
Flutter as birds adown the wold,

I may have run the glorious race,
  And caught the torch while yet aflame,
  And called upon the holy name
Of Him who now doth hide His face.

## AMY LEVY

# Ballade of an Omnibus

*'To see my love suffices me.'*
  – Ballades in Blue China.

Some men to carriages aspire;
On some the costly hansoms wait;
Some seek a fly, on job or hire;
Some mount the trotting steed, elate.
I envy not the rich and great,
A wandering minstrel, poor and free,
I am contented with my fate –
An omnibus suffices me.

In winter days of rain and mire
I find within a corner strait;
The 'busmen know me and my lyre
From Brompton to the Bull-and-Gate.
When summer comes, I mount in state
The topmost summit, whence I see
Croesus look up, compassionate –
An omnibus suffices me.

I mark, untroubled by desire,
Lucullus' phaeton and its freight.

The scene whereof I cannot tire,
The human tale of love and hate,
The city pageant, early and late
Unfolds itself, rolls by, to be
A pleasure deep and delicate.
An omnibus suffices me.

Princess, your splendour you require,
I, my simplicity; agree
Neither to rate lower nor higher.
An omnibus suffices me.

## JOHN GODFREY SAXE

# Railroad Rhyme

Singing through the forests,
Rattling over ridges;
Shooting under arches,
Rumbling over bridges;
Whizzing through the mountains,
Buzzing o'er the vale,
– Bless me! this is pleasant,
Riding on the rail!

Men of different 'stations'
In the eye of fame,
Here are very quickly
  Coming to the same;
High and lowly people,
Birds of every feather,
On a common level,
Travelling together.

Gentleman in shorts,
Looming very tall;

Gentleman at large
Talking very small;
Gentleman in tights,
    With a loose-ish mien;
Gentleman in gray,
Looking rather green;

Gentleman quite old,
Asking for the news;
Gentleman in black,
In a fit of blues;
Gentleman in claret,
Sober as a vicar;
Gentleman in tweed,
Dreadfully in liquor!

Stranger on the right
Looking very sunny,
Obviously reading
Something rather funny.
    Now the smiles are thicker, –
Wonder what they mean!
Faith, he's got the Knicker
Bocker Magazine!

Stranger on the left
Closing up his peepers;
Now he snores amain,
Like the Seven Sleepers;
At his feet a volume
Gives the explanation,
How the man grew stupid
From 'Association'!

Ancient maiden lady
Anxiously remarks,
That there must be peril
'Mong so many sparks;
Roguish-looking fellow,
Turning to the stranger,

Says it's his opinion
She is out of danger!

Woman with her baby,
Sitting vis-a-vis;
Baby keeps a-squalling,
Woman looks at me;
Asks about the distance,
Says it's tiresome talking,
Noises of the cars
Are so very shocking!

Market-woman, careful
Of the precious casket,
Knowing eggs are eggs,
Tightly holds her basket;
Feeling that a smash,
If it came, would surely
Send her eggs to pot,
Rather prematurely.

Singing through the forests,
Rattling over ridges;
Shooting under arches,
Rumbling over bridges;
Whizzing through the mountains
Buzzing o'er the vale,
Bless me! This is pleasant
Riding on the rail!

# MATTHEW ARNOLD

## Stanzas From the Grande Chartreuse

Through Alpine meadows soft-suffused
With rain, where thick the crocus blows,
Past the dark forges long disused,
The mule-track from Saint Laurent goes.
The bridge is cross'd, and slow we ride,
Through forest, up the mountain-side.

The autumnal evening darkens round,
The wind is up, and drives the rain;
While, hark! far down, with strangled sound
Doth the Dead Guier's stream complain,
Where that wet smoke, among the woods,
Over his boiling cauldron broods.

Swift rush the spectral vapours white
Past limestone scars with ragged pines,
Showing – then blotting from our sight! –
Halt – through the clod-drift something shines!
High in the valley, wet and drear,
The huts of Courrerie appear.

Strike leftward! cries our guide; and higher
Mounts up the stony forest-way.
At last the encircling trees retire;
Look! through the showery twilight grey
What pointed roofs are these advance? –
A palace of the Kings of France?

Approach, for what we seek is here!
Alight, and sparely sup, and wait
For rest in this outbuilding near;
Then cross the sward and reach that gate.
Knock; pass the wicket! Thou art come
To the Carthusians' world-famed home.

The silent courts, where night and day
Into their stone-carved basins cold
The splashing icy fountains play –
The humid corridors behold!
Where, ghostlike in the deepening night,
Cowl'd forms brush by in gleaming white.

The chapel, where no organ's peal
Invests the stern and naked prayer –
With penitential cries they kneel
And wrestle; rising then, with bare
And white uplifted faces stand,
Passing the Host from hand to hand;

Each takes, and then his visage wan
Is buried in his cowl once more.
The cells! – the suffering Son of Man
Upon the wall – the knee-worn floor –
And where they sleep, that wooden bed,
Which shall their coffin be, when dead!

The library, where tract and tome
Not to feed priestly pride are there,
To hymn the conquering march of Rome,
Nor yet to amuse, as ours are!
They paint of souls the inner strife,
Their drops of blood, their death in life.

The garden, overgrown – yet mild,
See, fragrant herbs are flowering there!
Strong children of the Alpine wild
Whose culture is the brethren's care;
Of human tasks their only one,
And cheerful works beneath the sun.

Those halls, too, destined to contain
Each its own pilgrim-host of old,
From England, Germany, or Spain –
All are before me! I behold
The House, the Brotherhood austere!
– And what am I, that I am here?

For rigorous teachers seized my youth,
And purged its faith, and trimm'd its fire,
Show'd me the high, white star of Truth,
There bade me gaze, and there aspire.
Even now their whispers pierce the gloom:
What dost thou in this living tomb?

Forgive me, masters of the mind!
At whose behest I long ago
So much unlearnt, so much resign'd –
I come not here to be your foe!
I seek these anchorites, not in ruth,
To curse and to deny your truth;

Not as their friend, or child, I speak!
But as, on some far northern strand,
Thinking of his own Gods, a Greek
In pity and mournful awe might stand
Before some fallen Runic stone –
For both were faiths, and both are gone.

Wandering between two worlds, one dead,
The other powerless to be born,
With nowhere yet to rest my head,
Like these, on earth I wait forlorn.
Their faith, my tears, the world deride –
I come to shed them at their side.

Oh, hide me in your gloom profound,
Ye solemn seats of holy pain!
Take me, cowl'd forms, and fence me round,
Till I possess my soul again;
Till free my thoughts before me roll,
Not chafed by hourly false control!

For the world cries your faith is now
But a dead time's exploded dream;
My melancholy, sciolists say,

Is a pass'd mode, an outworn theme –
As if the world had ever had
A faith, or sciolists been sad!

Ah, if it be pass'd, take away,
At least, the restlessness, the pain;
Be man henceforth no more a prey
To these out-dated stings again!
The nobleness of grief is gone
Ah, leave us not the fret alone!

But – if you cannot give us ease –
Last of the race of them who grieve
Here leave us to die out with these
Last of the people who believe!
Silent, while years engrave the brow;
Silent – the best are silent now.

Achilles ponders in his tent,
The kings of modern thought are dumb,
Silent they are though not content,
And wait to see the future come.
They have the grief men had of yore,
But they contend and cry no more.

Our fathers water'd with their tears
This sea of time whereon we sail,
Their voices were in all men's ears
We pass'd within their puissant hail.
Still the same ocean round us raves,
But we stand mute, and watch the waves.

For what avail'd it, all the noise
And outcry of the former men? –
Say, have their sons achieved more joys,
Say, is life lighter now than then?
The sufferers died, they left their pain –
The pangs which tortured them remain.

What helps it now, that Byron bore,
With haughty scorn which mock'd the smart,
Through Europe to the Atolian shore
The pageant of his bleeding heart?
That thousands counted every groan,
And Europe made his woe her own?

What boots it, Shelley! that the breeze
Carried thy lovely wail away,
Musical through Italian trees
Which fringe thy soft blue Spezzian bay?
Inheritors of thy distress
Have restless hearts one throb the less?

Or are we easier, to have read,
O Obermann! the sad, stern page,
Which tells us how thou hidd'st thy head
From the fierce tempest of thine age
In the lone brakes of Fontainebleau,
Or chalets near the Alpine snow?

Ye slumber in your silent grave! –
The world, which for an idle day
Grace to your mood of sadness gave,
Long since hath flung her weeds away.
The eternal trifler breaks your spell;
But we – we learned your lore too well!

Years hence, perhaps, may dawn an age,
More fortunate, alas! than we,
Which without hardness will be sage,
And gay without frivolity.
Sons of the world, oh, speed those years;
But, while we wait, allow our tears!

Allow them! We admire with awe
The exulting thunder of your race;
You give the universe your law,
You triumph over time and space!
Your pride of life, your tireless powers,
We laud them, but they are not ours.

We are like children rear'd in shade
Beneath some old-world abbey wall,
Forgotten in a forest-glade,
And secret from the eyes of all.
Deep, deep the greenwood round them waves,
Their abbey, and its close of graves!

But, where the road runs near the stream,
Oft through the trees they catch a glance
Of passing troops in the sun's beam –
Pennon, and plume, and flashing lance!
Forth to the world those soldiers fare,
To life, to cities, and to war!

And through the wood, another way,
Faint bugle-notes from far are borne,
Where hunters gather, staghounds bay,
Round some fair forest-lodge at morn.
Gay dames are there, in sylvan green;
Laughter and cries – those notes between!

The banners flashing through the trees
Make their blood dance and chain their eyes;
That bugle-music on the breeze
Arrests them with a charm'd surprise.
Banner by turns and bugle woo:
Ye shy recluses, follow too!

O children, what do ye reply? –
'Action and pleasure, will ye roam
Through these secluded dells to cry
And call us? – but too late ye come!
Too late for us your call ye blow,
Whose bent was taken long ago.

'Long since we pace this shadow'd nave;
We watch those yellow tapers shine,
Emblems of hope over the grave,
In the high altar's depth divine;
The organ carries to our ear
Its accents of another sphere.

'Fenced early in this cloistral round
Of reverie, of shade, of prayer,
How should we grow in other ground?
How can we flower in foreign air?
– Pass, banners, pass, and bugles, cease;
And leave our desert to its peace!'


## ROBERT LOUIS STEVENSON

# To an Island Princess

Since long ago, a child at home,
I read and longed to rise and roam,
Where'er I went, whate'er I willed,
One promised land my fancy filled.
Hence the long roads my home I made;
Tossed much in ships; have often laid
Below the uncurtained sky my head,
Rain-deluged and wind-buffeted:
And many a thousand hills I crossed
And corners turned – Love's labour lost,
Till, Lady, to your isle of sun
I came, not hoping; and, like one
Snatched out of blindness, rubbed my eyes,
And hailed my promised land with cries.

Yes, Lady, here I was at last;
Here found I all I had forecast:
The long roll of the sapphire sea
That keeps the land's virginity;
The stalwart giants of the wood
Laden with toys and flowers and food;
The precious forest pouring out
To compass the whole town about;

The town itself with streets of lawn,
Loved of the moon, blessed by the dawn,
Where the brown children all the day
Keep up a ceaseless noise of play,
Play in the sun, play in the rain,
Nor ever quarrel or complain;
– And late at night, in the woods of fruit,
Hark! do you hear the passing flute?
I threw one look to either hand,
And knew I was in Fairyland.
And yet one point of being so
I lacked. For, Lady (as you know),
Whoever by his might of hand,
Won entrance into Fairyland,
Found always with admiring eyes
A Fairy princess kind and wise.
It was not long I waited; soon
Upon my threshold, in broad noon,
Gracious and helpful, wise and good,
The Fairy Princess Moe stood.

## ROBERT LOUIS STEVENSON

# To Kalakaua

### (With a present of a Pearl)

The Silver Ship, my King – that was her name
In the bright islands whence your fathers came –
The Silver Ship, at rest from winds and tides,
Below your palace in your harbour rides:
And the seafarers, sitting safe on shore,
Like eager merchants count their treasures o'er.
One gift they find, one strange and lovely thing,
Now doubly precious since it pleased a king.

The right, my liege, is ancient as the lyre
For bards to give to kings what kings admire.
'Tis mine to offer for Apollo's sake;
And since the gift is fitting, yours to take.
To golden hands the golden pearl I bring:
The ocean jewel to the island king.


## ROBERT LOUIS STEVENSON

# To Princess Kaiulani

[Written in April to Kaiulani in the April of her age; and at Waikiki, within easy walk of Kaiulani's banyan! When she comes to my land and her father's, and the rain beats upon the window (as I fear it will), let her look at this page; it will be like a weed gathered and pressed at home; and she will remember her own islands, and the shadow of the mighty tree; and she will hear the peacocks screaming in the dusk and the wind blowing in the palms; and she will think of her father sitting there alone. – R. L. S.]

Forth from her land to mine she goes,
The island maid, the island rose,
Light of heart and bright of face:
The daughter of a double race.

Her islands here, in Southern sun,
Shall mourn their Kaiulani gone,
And I, in her dear banyan shade,
Look vainly for my little maid.

But our Scots islands far away
Shall glitter with unwonted day,
And cast for once their tempests by
To smile in Kaiulani's eye.

## ROBERT LOUIS STEVENSON

# To My Wife

### (A Fragment)

Long must elapse ere you behold again
Green forest frame the entry of the lane –
The wild lane with the bramble and the brier,
The year-old cart-tracks perfect in the mire,
The wayside smoke, perchance, the dwarfish huts,
And ramblers' donkey drinking from the ruts: –
Long ere you trace how deviously it leads,
Back from man's chimneys and the bleating meads
To the woodland shadow, to the sylvan hush,
When but the brooklet chuckles in the brush –
Back from the sun and bustle of the vale
To where the great voice of the nightingale
Fills all the forest like a single room,
And all the banks smell of the golden broom;
So wander on until the eve descends.
And back returning to your firelit friends,
You see the rosy sun, despoiled of light,
Hung, caught in thickets, like a schoolboy's kite.
Here from the sea the unfruitful sun shall rise,
Bathe the bare deck and blind the unshielded eyes;
The allotted hours aloft shall wheel in vain
And in the unpregnant ocean plunge again.
Assault of squalls that mock the watchful guard,
And pluck the bursting canvas from the yard,
And senseless clamour of the calm, at night
Must mar your slumbers. By the plunging light,
In beetle-haunted, most unwomanly bower
Of the wild-swerving cabin, hour by hour . . .